Mind the Light

Learning to See with Spiritual Eyes

J. BRENT BILL

PARACLETE PRESS
BREWSTER, MASSACHUSETTS

Mind the Light: Learning to See with Spiritual Eyes

2006   First Printing

Copyright 2006 by J. Brent Bill

ISBN 1-55725-489-3

Library of Congress Cataloging-in-Publication Data
Bill, J. Brent, 1951-
Mind the light : learning to see with spiritual eyes / J. Brent Bill.
    p. cm.   Includes bibliographical references.
ISBN 1-55725-489-3
1. Spiritual life--Christianity. 2. Spirituality.
3. Meditation. 4. Contemplation. I. Title.
BV4501.3.B495 2006   248.4'6--dc22

                                                                        2006014533

10 9 8 7 6 5 4 3 2 1

Published by Paraclete Press
Brewster, Massachusetts
www.paracletepress.com

Printed in the United States of America

To Nancy
Here lies a she sun, and a he moon there,
She gives the best light to his sphere
—John Donne

CONTENTS

Sunflowers and Souls

Light: Without it we die. Physically. Spiritually. Our very lives depend on light for photosynthesis—energy from sunlight that converts into adenosine triphosphate (ATP), the fuel used by all living things. That's why sunflowers track the sun across the sky, sea otters bask while floating in the ocean, and I look for an excuse to go to Florida in January. All God's creatures move toward the light—flowers, trees, people. Light is constant and ever present. At least that's what we assume. Then the power goes out or a month of clouds rolls in. We grumble and moan and whine until the light comes back.

But even more than physically, we respond to illumination emotionally and spiritually. Light—depending on its strength, tone, slant—changes how we perceive the world and people. Light sets a Midwestern sunset apart from a Western desert sunset, a Goya portrait from a John Singer Sargent portrait, and a joyful spirit apart from a mournful one. Yet even though light is all around us, we often don't notice it and the difference it can make in our souls. That's where an old Quaker saying—"Mind the Light"—offers help. "Mind" in this case means many things—including heed, tend, notice, observe, and obey. Minding the Light is a way of deep seeing.

I need help seeing. I've been nearsighted since high school and joined the bifocaled folks when I turned forty. I'm also diabetic. That means I go to my optometrist annually and have my eyes thoroughly checked. At a recent examination, Dr. Groninger talked me into trying contact lenses.

I liked the immediate results. I looked days younger with them—so much younger I considered getting a toupee and dyeing my beard. But I had trouble reading. I saw faraway stuff. But not near. The first day I went out to lunch with people from the office and picked up the check. That's about all I did, because I couldn't read it. I had to trust a coworker to fill in the amount for the tip.

So I went back to the doctor. She made an adjustment. Much better. I could read. But then I started driving. My distance was blurrier. Another week and I was back. "What do you think?" Dr. Groninger asked. "Well, I like not messing with glasses. I like the freedom. But I'm still having trouble—now it's distance." "Let's try modified monovision." She explained that she was going to power up my left eye for reading and my right eye for distance. "Oh, we're going to trick my brain, huh?"

"Not really," she said. Then she explained that sight already tricks our brains. We favor one eye over the other all the time, based on what our needs are. If we're in a concert and someone with a big hat sits in front of us, the eye that can see the show tells the brain, "Hey, pay attention here and forget that hat." And we do. So now I'm learning to see in a new way and tell my brain what to pay attention to.

The poet Tess Gallagher writes:

> My father loved first light.
> He would sit alone
> at the yellow formica table
> in the kitchen with his coffee cup
> and sip and look out . . .
>
> My father picks up his
> cup. Light is sifting in
> like a gloam of certainty
> over the water. He knows
> something there in the half light
> he can't know any other way.

That's what *Mind the Light* is about: A way to learn things in the light, whether at Formica tables with coffee cups or quietly reading a spiritual memoir or in the middle of our workaday world. Minding the Light adds a further dimension to eyes and brain: our souls. It helps us pay attention to God's Light around us and in us. How we see our lives changes as this illumination leads us to a deep appreciation of the soulful things of life. Minding the Light is an invitation to experience a new way of seeing that shows our brains and souls what to pay attention to. It's a way of seeing our inner and outer lives with spiritual eyes and discovering the connectedness between inner and outer sight.

Throughout *Mind the Light* you'll encounter boxed text labeled "Illuminating Moments." These are meant as brief exercises in Minding the Light. Illuminating Moments are based on the Quaker practice of asking Queries. The

Religious Society of Friends (as Quakers are officially known) have used Queries for almost 350 years as a way to examine our souls, seek clarity, and gain spiritual insight. Queries are a practice that can be used by anyone looking for God's Light in life. The Illuminating Moments in this book are not about mystical experiences of God, though they may occur. As you read the Illuminating Moments, let your mind and soul fill with words, ideas, or images. Using the Light of God inside and outside you, look deeply into the Holy.

Learning to Mind the Light is CPR for the soul. It's an encounter that will save your light.

CHAPTER ONE

Minding the Light
The Spirituality of Seeing

Four points of golden light shone back especially bright. "What do you think they are?" asked my wife, Nancy, as she relaxed in the passenger seat after a late supper. I had flipped on my high beams after turning up our driveway late one night. The light shone the fifteen-hundred-foot length of the graveled lane and into the woods at the end. "Probably squirrels. Could be coyotes," I answered, flicking the beams on low. "Let's find out." As we pulled into the garage and shut the lights off, I grabbed the portable searchlight my dad had given me for Christmas. Nancy made her way into the house and I went to sit on the front steps. Flipping the searchlight on, one million candlepower shot across the field in front of our house (when we say "let there be light," we mean let there be lotsa light). I moved the beam slowly and picked up more golden points of light. As I focused on the shining eyes, the forms of four deer swam into view out of the nighttime ground fog. The deer looked away, moved a few steps, and then looked back up at the light. Nancy came out, leaned over, and whispered, "What is it?" I nodded down the light beam. She smiled and settled in next to me. "Beautiful," she sighed. I nodded. We watched the deer for about fifteen minutes, moving, grazing, looking at the light, moving, grazing, looking at the light. A car passed on the road, its muffler needing repair. The deer started, then raced across the field, and leapt into the woods.

Later, thinking about those deer, I remembered other nights I'd shone the light across the field, picking up squirrels' and rabbits' eyes. One night I lit up a pack of coyotes. They didn't turn away from the light. They looked straight at it. Two of them even began racing toward the light. As they did, I snapped off the searchlight and ran inside. I grew up a city boy—what do I know from coyotes?

That deer and coyotes turned toward the light shouldn't surprise me. Our former feline Stephanie Vandercatten used to move her lazy, lithe, Siamese body from spot to spot in the living room following the sun's rays passing through the windows. I turn the plants on my office desk so that the leaves don't all grow toward the window, leaving a bunch of stalks for me to gaze at. Even free-range plants—black-eyed Susans, daisy fleabane, spiderwort—stretch toward the sun. The most blatant examples of plants' moving toward sunlight are sunflowers, which relentlessly follow the sun, turning their heads to track the sun each day across the sky.

All creation seeks the light. When the sun breaks through after a stretch of cloudy winter days, the people in our office stand and gaze through our large windows at the courtyard bathed in brightness. When folks in Indiana sign up for winter vacations, they're not usually heading to Canada's Northwest Territories—they're off to someplace sunny.

We laugh about some folks being sun worshipers, but our moods are better and so is our health when we soak up some sun. Even a fair-skinned bald guy like me enjoys the feel of the sun and feels better for being out in it. I can tell when Nancy's been working outside on a sunny day just by the way she smells—she has what I think of as the scent of the sun. It's a pretty attractive aroma.

ILLUMINATING MOMENT
Breathe deeply.
Relax your body and mind.
Think about the following slowly and gently.
Savor each thought.
Have I ever smelled or felt or tasted or heard light?
What were those sensations?

Humans are solar powered: The St. Petersburg/ Clearwater Area Convention and Visitors Bureau advertises its sunny climate with that phrase. But it's more than some outrageous advertising claim; they're right. The energy that beats in our hearts originates in the core of the sun. It's pretty complex and I don't fully understand it, but I do know that there is a link from nuclear fusion in the sun to the energy released by our cells. Vitamin D from sunlight also helps protect against lymphoma and cancers of the prostate, lung, colon, and skin. Exposure to bright light in the morning boosts energy levels throughout the day.

"One reason for the fatigue that is rampant in our society may be light deprivation," says Michael Terman. Terman is director of clinical chronobiology (in short, the study of the rhythms of our bodily functions) at the New York State Psychiatric Institute in New York City. His research suggests that exposure to bright light in the morning boosts energy levels throughout the day. Terman and other scientists aren't exactly sure why, but they think it may be because light stimulates neurotransmitters in our brains. Now I know a little bit more about neurotransmitters than I do about coyotes. I know this because I take a medicine that improves the response of a neurotransmitter called serotonin. Serotonin and other neurotransmitters improve mood and increase motivation.

According to the studies, while exposure to any sunlight provides a little boost, "the dawn signal" (as Terman calls it) is particularly beneficial. I think the strength of this signal depends on the person—Nancy's reception to the dawn signal is much stronger than mine. This probably has something to do with my so rarely being awake at dawn. It turns out that taking a morning walk or stepping out to Starbucks for an AM cuppa joe on even a cloudy day offers enough light to have a stimulating effect on the brain. Our bodies crave light.

So do our souls. Springing from deep within our spirits, this yearning for light is more than physical. It is also a yearning for God. The Bible tells us that "God is light; in him is no darkness at all." When I think about that, I understand a bit more clearly why my desire for light carries me closer to God. I am hungering for a connection to the divine. God is light. God made light. Light invites me into the presence of the divine. The Light of the divine presence remakes me in ways that are restrained and not so restrained. Sometimes it's through a gentle stirring of love. At other times it is in a flash of revelation. That may sound mystical and radical. But, then, perhaps we don't have quite enough mystery and radicalness in our daily lives to feed our spirits adequately. Maybe we're not getting enough of our recommended daily allowance of spiritual light.

Nancy and I take a train trip to Washington, D.C., every time one of our grandchildren turns ten. Usually we take the young person with us. Since I am a one-time art major, one of my favorite things is to visit the National Gallery. My stated goal is to introduce our grand-offspring to the glories of fine art. On a recent trip, we stopped in front of Jean Siméon Chardin's "Fruit, Jug, and a Glass." Painted around 1755, it is a stunning study of light—on a jug and fruit and shining through a glass of water. I was trying to explain to my grandson how Chardin worked his alchemy of bringing oil paint to light. I ran out of adequate words. I couldn't find a way to express how deeply this subtle use of sunlight moved me. As I stood there I was amazed at how his artist's eye captured the splendor of everyday items in such a way that more than two hundred years later I was transfixed by his vision. This led me inside to a quiet moment of praise for the God who created both Chardin's artistic ability and the light that inspired his painting. I tried to say something to Austin, but finally gave up. He just looked up at me, smiled, said, "Cool, huh?" and turned back to look at the picture with me, standing just a bit closer to me than before.

Every one of us experiences powerful moments like that one, and they feed our souls. If we take time to look back at them, we find that many of them are filled with light, whether it was looking at a piece of art, standing under a heavenly host of stars that caused our hearts to murmur, "Glory to God in the highest," or watching a child's face brighten with the surprise of an unexpected present. These experiences reveal the call our spirits feel to the light. Johann Wolfgang von Goethe recognized this when he wrote:

Were the eye not of the sun,
How could we behold the light?
If God's might and ours were not as one,
How could His work enchant our sight?

Light, more than some physical fact or phenomenon, calls us to the holy. Artists throughout time have been good at seeing that connection. Hildegard of Bingen, the great twelfth-century German mystic-artist, described an artist as a person ". . . who can say God has illumined me in both eyes. By them I behold the splendor of light in the darkness."

The ability of being illumined in both eyes—the eyes of our body and of our soul—makes it possible to feel a sublime connection to the divine. That's why Paul Cézanne said, "When I judge art, I take my painting and put it next to a God-made object like a tree or flower. If it clashes, it is not art." God's realism is the ultimate reality. Artists—painters, sculptors, musicians—have long known that being attuned to the light, the ability to see deeply, connects us with the holy in a fresh and new way. To each of us, Minding the Light opens the artists' way of seeing. As we Mind the Light, our souls open to receive the gifts of God in the same way a morning glory opens to greet the dawn.

ILLUMINATING MOMENT
Breathe deeply.
Relax your body and mind.
Think about the following slowly and gently.
Savor each thought.
When have I felt my soul open in response to light?

I am reminded of this every time I sing one of my favorite hymns, "Immortal, Invisible, God Only Wise." Written by Walter Chalmers Smith, a pastor in the Free Church of Scotland, it contains a powerful line that captures the essence of God—"Unresting, unhasting, and silent as light." Every time I join a group of Sunday-morning singers launching into that hymn—even if some of them are off-key and I'm singing flat—I reflect on what that line tells me about God and about light. One is that light is unresting—light never turns off the light. It shines on and keeps on shining. Another is that it's not hurried. We all know that light is fast. It travels at 299,792,458 meters per second. Science also says that that's a constant speed. Unlike my MG on the back roads, which sometimes goes forty-five or sixty-five and sometimes goes . . . well, forget about that, light is steady. It is unhasting—not rushing.

Finally, Smith reminds me that light is silent. That appeals to the Quaker in me. But his words make another point. Light is not heard—it is seen. So much of our sensory experience is based in surround sound or the presence of a soundtrack in our lives. In the movie *As Good As It Gets*, Jack Nicholson's character, Melvin, heads out on a road trip with CDs labeled for all occasions—even one stashed in the glove box titled "In Case of Emergency." When I look at my own 200-plus CD collection (sorted alphabetically by artist and then by release date), I see how easily I could be like Melvin and try to fill every moment with a soundtrack. While that might be okay for him, a day, or a life, filled with preplanned music would make it too easy for me to miss seeing God's Light.

That's because light doesn't shout. Occasionally it hums if a fluorescent fixture needs fixing, but most of the time light flows over and around us while not calling attention to itself. Since light is silent, if I want to notice it I have to be silent, too. I can't really pay attention when I'm noisy. My attention is diverted or distracted by sound—whether CDs for every occasion or a conversation between coworkers in the hall. The kind of seeing that feeds my soul means I have to pay attention. If I don't, then I move into a sensory over-load mode where the immediacy of life and what is going on around me blinds me to the subtle influences of the spirit. My eyes are still functioning, along with my ears, and nose, and fingers, but to see the Light, I must find space to pay attention—if, that is, I want to move beyond seeing and into beholding. That's a word we don't hear often. The word *behold* reminds some of us of childhood Christmas pageants where we dressed up in old bathrobes and marched onstage to play shepherds and wise men while the prettiest girl in fourth grade swept onstage dressed in a white gown and proclaimed, "Behold, I bring you good tidings of great joy."

Behold is a good, if unused, word. *Behold* implies a depth of seeing that's beyond the ordinary. It means taking a really good look. I can be in a crowded room and see lots of people, but when Nancy comes in, I behold her. She's the love of my life, and the sight of her continues to bring me joy. Beholding is how we see someone or something that we love dearly and that brings joy into our lives. The artist Alex Grey says, "In the act of deeply seeing, we transcend the boundaries between the self and the otherness of the world, momentarily merging with the thing seen." So when we behold and take a really good look, we somehow blur our separateness and become one with the other person. Perhaps this happens in the same way (less physical, but just as mystical) that sex blends two bodies into one for an eternal instant. To think of it this way is to charge seeing with an intimacy we don't usually experience. Yet, that sort of depth of experience is when the light—the sight—breaks through. Beholding leads us to an intimate encounter with God.

ILLUMINATING MOMENT
Breathe deeply.
Relax your body and mind.
Think about the following slowly and gently.
Savor each thought.
When is a time that I have beheld a light charged with a divine intimacy?

Everything we experience in this life—plants, animals, each other—was created after light was. Yes, God is light, but paradoxically, light is also among the first things God made. "And God said, 'Let there be light,' and there was light. God saw that the light was good." One of the things about God's creating light that I didn't catch for a long time was that "God made two great lights—the greater light to govern the day and the lesser light to govern the night." Yes, I knew there were a sun and a moon. I'd read that Bible verse many times. But I had never picked up on the significance of the part about two great lights. Once I did, I came to love the phrases "greater light" and "lesser light." Part of that eye-opening enjoyment came from seeing that, concerning these "great" lights, "God saw that [they were] good."

The idea that both kinds of light—daylight and nightlight—are good was something new for me. I grew up in the city. There we tried to defeat the nightlight by overpowering it—streetlamps, patio lights, mercury lights, road lamps, freeway lamps—each adding more and more light. I remember the first time we drove toward our home in Columbus, Ohio, on a cloudy evening and saw the underside of the clouds aglow with light reflected from the city below. The effect was cool, but spooky at the same time. Even as a kid I thought this scene seemed unnatural.

One of the things I've learned since moving to the country this time is the goodness of the nightlight. Many people love moonlit walks, but my first real experience of this nightlight came when I walked down our long lane over to Nancy's dad's nearby house. Nancy spent many hours there taking care of her father during the last few years of his life. A night helper often came to relieve her around ten PM. Some nights I would hike over and walk Nancy home. One fall night the moon was full, so I left my flashlight at home. That night, as I walked along, with just a bit of nip in the air, the stone driveway shone silver. The moon was so bright that the trees cast flickering shadows across my path. Stars glittered in the sky and the world seemed at sleepy peace. It fed my soul—a soft light moving gentle stirrings inside me of gratitude and grace. For the first time I felt as if I understood that all of God's light is good. It's easy for me to see the daylight as good—that's the light that shines on the flowers, in my grandkids' eyes, and lights my way as I drive my tractor across the field. It takes a bit more beholding on my part to recognize that nightlight is beautiful and illuminating in its own worthy way. Things are dimmer. Less focused. Softer. All of which are good things, but I don't usually notice them as I flip on the high beams of my life while rushing through the darkness from one point of brilliant light to another. That night the old Quaker phrase "Mind the Light" came alive to me.

Now, when Friends use this phrase, we usually mean that we are to pay attention to the movement of God in our souls. The word *mind* in that expression means "pay attention to" or "heed" the light—not *mind* as in "be bothered by." Before Friends called themselves Friends they referred to themselves as the "Children of Light." They warmed to the spiritual idea of the immediacy of Christ's presence preached by a young man named George Fox. He spoke of "Christ within" each person, a presence he called the "Inner Light." That's based on John's saying that "the true light,

which enlightens everyone, was coming into the world"—
referring to Jesus as the true Light. From Fox's preaching
and their reading of the Bible, the early Quakers understood
Jesus to be the Light of the world. They referred to Christ
as the Inner Light alive inside everybody. They also chose
the name "Children of Light" because they wanted people
to know that they were walking in the Light of God. Their
name came from John's Gospel that says, "While you
have the light, believe in the light, so that you may
become [children] of light." They wanted to be known as
women and men whose faith grew from a direct spiritual
encounter with the living Light of Christ. They believed this
Light was present in every spiritual seeker as an inward
guide and teacher. So they invited others to experience the
Light. Experiencing the Light was absolutely fundamental
to their witness. They felt that they were the people that the
prophet Isaiah had talked about—"A people that walked in
darkness has seen a great light." They urged themselves and
others to, as the writer of Ephesians says, "[Walk] as children
of light . . . for the fruit of the light is found in all that is good
and right and true."

Friends still believe that the Light of God shines within
each person. This *Light Within* is more than intellect or
conscience. The Light Within is like a flickering flame
implanted deep in our souls that, when responded to and
tended in love, grows to fill our entire lives with light.
Minding the Light then helps us live with integrity and follow
God as best as we can.

While certainly not a Quaker, Thomas Merton experienced the feeling of Minding the Light. In *The Seven Storey*

Mountain, recalling his experience of the amazingly paradoxical immanence and transcendence of God as light, he writes:

> It was a light that was so bright that it had no relation to visible light and so profound and so intimate that it seemed like a neutralization of every lesser experience. And yet the thing that struck me most of all was that this light was in a certain sense ordinary—it was a light (and this was most of all what took my breath away)—that was offered to all, to everybody, and there was nothing fancy or strange about it. It was the light of faith deepened and reduced to an extreme and sudden obviousness.

ILLUMINATING MOMENT
Breathe deeply.
Relax your body and mind.
Think about the following slowly and gently.
Savor each thought.
Have I ever experienced light that was ordinary and profound?

A light that is bright, profound, intimate, and ordinary while being beyond ordinary is something Danish architect Jørn Utzon works toward. Utzon designed the Sydney Opera House with its evocation of sails, shells, and gull wings. His work with light moves from the inward focus of the

Quakers and Merton to outer light. He says that the effect
he is looking for in his work is that of seeing a Gothic
church. "You never finish with it while you move around it
or see it against the sky. This interplay with the sun, the
light, the clouds is so important that it makes the building
into a living thing." This idea that light moving around a
structure can imbue it with life may seem a bit of a stretch—
or a bit spiritual. Yet, while the skeptic in me says, "Sure,"
the soul of me, intrigued, begins to look at how light plays
around the very room in which I'm reading those lines. It's
early evening; the sun is setting in the west, and casting a
thinning golden light into the trees to the east of the
house, which is in turn reflected back through the two-story
windows into the living room where I'm sitting. As the light
lowers in the west and climbs the eastern trees, it moves
through the living room—shining now on the clinker-brick
hearth, scaling the wooden posts, and illuminating the paper
needlework "Welcome" sign resting on the mantle. The room
feels alive with memories of the mason who laid each of
the clinker bricks for the forty-foot-high chimney, the
crew that set the posts and beams framing our house, and
Nancy's great-grandmother who carefully pierced paper
with thread to welcome friends to her home.

A simple, rectangular building with gray, horizontally
sided walls and white trim on West 26th Street in Houston,
Texas, is another place where holy light plays. From the outside, Live Oaks Friends Meetinghouse, designed by the artist
James Turrell, hardly seems to be a space conceived around the
concept of being able to Mind the Light well and intentionally.
The interior doesn't give any immediate clues, either, as it

consists of an area for people to gather to visit prior to worship, another area with bathrooms and a table for meetings, and the meeting room. The meeting room is square, with plain plaster walls and tall windows. Worshipers sit on plain, white oak benches that Turrell designed. Then there's the high, vaulted ceiling. That's where the "skyspace" is—a twelve-by twelve-foot square opening at the apex of the curved ceiling. The skyspace offers a view of the sky's changing character and light, all in a spiritual setting. It's as if an unresting, unhasting, and silent panorama of light and art is unfolding over anyone who would take time to look up through it. Turrell, a Quaker, said, "I guess I like the literal quality, or feeling, or sensation, in that I want to feel light physically. We drink it as vitamin D; it's actually a food. . . . We also have a big psychological relation to light. All or most spiritual experiences . . . are described with a vocabulary of light."

"We generally use [light] to illuminate other things," James Turrell has said, "but I wanted to force people to pay attention to the thingness and revelation of light."

This paying attention to the "thingness" and revelation of light is suggested by the concept of Minding the Light. Turrell's words remind us that light has substance—as does God. There's a *there* there. Light is good simply because it is—light is one of God's creations, the same as birds, bees, sunflowers, coyotes, and us. Because light is also revelatory it shows us things as well as thingness. Light enlivens us to the world around us, enabling us to see with spiritual eyes both God and God's creation.

"Light I acknowledge as the energy upon which all life on this planet depends," said photographer Ruth Bernhard, who turned one hundred years old in 2005. "Light is my inspiration, my paint and brush. It is as vital as the model herself. Profoundly significant, it caresses the essential superlative curves and lines."

> ILLUMINATING MOMENT
> Breathe deeply.
> Relax your body and mind.
> Think about the following slowly and gently.
> Savor each thought.
> *How would I describe the "thingness" of divine Light?*

It's easy to miss the light—to not see it. A good friend and I were driving across Indiana recently when she looked out the window and asked, "What are you seeing?" On another, earlier trip she'd asked that question while we were deep in conversation about landscape and light. I'd waxed eloquent about the qualities of light that lit fields filled with corn stubble and that had illuminated the soft contours of Midwestern rolling ground. I had spoken eloquently enough, at least, so that she seemed to enjoy the conversation and my view on things that she didn't seem to see with her hillier, woodier New England eyes.

Her question stopped me cold. I looked around. I saw a not-too-unusual cloudy Indiana day in the middle of harvest. Some fields were picked. Some were not. I began to explain how to tell the difference between corn and bean fields, combine corn heads and bean heads, and . . . I knew I was stalling. I wasn't seeing anything much different from what she saw. I was embarrassed. Disappointed. Here I was writing a book about light and seeing and spirituality and I felt blind.

"Oh, Metamora," I said, changing the subject. "You've got to see it," pulling off the highway. We drove slowly through the once thriving canal town, now a tiny arts and crafts haven. As we moved back out onto the highway, I wondered why I couldn't see in the way she expected me to. Then it hit me. I wasn't paying attention in love to the landscape. Instead, I was paying attention to my friend and our conversation about books and writers. Paying attention in love was something I'd been thinking about a lot. Two weeks earlier I'd heard Michael Lindvall, the pastor of the Brick Presbyterian Church in Manhattan, and author of *Leaving North Haven*, say that one of the things that helped him write carefully crafted fiction about congregational life was that he had two things going for him—attention and love. That concept, he said, came from a fellow named Belden Lane. "Take a look at his writing on this," Lindvall urged me. "It will make your writing stronger."

So I did. In looking at his writing and reading about Lane himself, I found that he is a humanities professor in the theology department at Saint Louis University. Though I'm a seminary graduate, I've never thought of the theology department as a place for inspiration on landscape and light. Yet, Lane surprised me. He brought his theological eye together with his aesthetic one and said that in order to see the presence of God, two things are needed: attention and love. I was a bit skeptical about this, because Lane is also the man who wrote, "I'd heard that Quakers have as many words for silence as Eskimos do for snow"—and I know that isn't true! Still, his idea of attention and love intrigued me. So I read some of his books and articles. That's when I came across these thoughts:

> One begins to suspect that the contemplation of any ordinary thing, made extraordinary by attention and love, can become an occasion for glimpsing the profound. Lewis Thomas finds hope for the human species in the accumulative intelligence of termites, the thrush in his backyard, and a protozoan named *Myxotricha paradoxa.* He simply attends with the eye of a biologist to what passes beneath our senses every day. G. K. Chesterton once suggested that "it is a good exercise, in empty or ugly hours of the day, to look at anything, the coal-scuttle or the book-case, and think how happy one could be to have brought it out of the sinking ship onto the solitary island" (*Orthodoxy* [Fontana. 1961]. p. 63). Such an exercise can be no small aid in attaching true value to the most commonplace of things around us.
>
> Where can I not encounter the holy, has been the question of spiritual writers in every tradition and every age. "Whither shall I go from thy Spirit? Or whither shall I flee from thy presence?" asked the psalmist (139:7). Once our attention is brought to focus on the masked extraordinariness of things, we are hard put in to discern the allegedly profane.

That's when I realized that while riding with my friend, I don't have unlimited reserves of attention. Attention is different from love, in that way. We humans have limitless amounts of love. We can love many people in many types of ways—our children, parents, spouses, friends, ourselves—and nobody is poorer for the love we have for the others. Attention is different. I was unable to see anything outside because I was watching her and our conversation with attention and love. I had love for the landscape; I just couldn't pay attention to her and it at the same time.

Still, something unusual happened that day. By her asking the question, and my thinking about it, I soon began listening to our conversation *and* looking at the world beyond the car and the rain-soaked road. And I remembered one of my favorite quotations by Pierre Lacout, a former Catholic priest and Carmelite monk, who'd become a Quaker. Lacout said, "In silence which is active, the Inner Light begins to glow—a tiny spark. For the flame to be kindled and to grow, subtle argument and the clamor of our emotions must be stilled. It is by an attention full of love that we enable the Inner Light to blaze and illuminate our dwelling and to make of our whole being a source from which this Light may shine out."

The landscape whizzed by, but I saw it more slowly than the sixty-five miles per hour we were going. I found myself paying attention at a different level with everything going on around me. The outer and inner lights seemed brighter. All this was thanks to my friend's question.

ILLUMINATING MOMENT
Breathe deeply.
Relax your body and mind.
Think about the following slowly and gently.
Savor each thought.
How would I begin to look with attention and love?

Seeing with attention and love takes us to a place where the things of this world and our lives are limned—either brightly or dimly—with a spiritual beauty that leads us to the divine and sparks our imagination and spirit. It's a place that calls to us from deep in our souls. It's a place that leads from light to even more light—a light shining with brightness, profundity, and intimacy.

CHAPTER TWO

✳

The Light Around Us
Seeing Creation

"Look at the light," urged Jerry Bontrager. Jerry
was my art professor at Wilmington College. Short, dark-
haired, with intense eyes and an artistic soul, Jerry always
implored me to see more than what appeared to be there.
Not that I needed much encouragement. I'd been interested
in art long before I declared myself an art major at
Wilmington. As a teenager, I'd fancied myself the Monet or
Manet of West High School. Robert McLinn, the art teacher
there, while hardly indulging my fantasy, did encourage my
attempts—both artistic and artless. He shepherded me and
other Art League members on field trips to art museums and
working artists' studios in Columbus. He entered some of
my paintings in public school student competitions, where
they did well enough to garner a prize or two. Later, while at
Chatfield College, a small Ursuline school in southwestern
Ohio, Father Bob, the professor of painting, took me further
into the art world. In college, I still fancied myself a water-
colorist, but I had also rediscovered a love of photography
that began with my first Instamatic camera in 1966. Father
Bob encouraged both painting and darkroom experiments. In
doing so, he introduced me to light in art in new ways.

Like Bob McLinn, Father Bob took us on lots of field trips. One was to a commercial photography studio where they were shooting an ice-cream advertisement. While we were there, the photographer explained his various lighting techniques—tungsten versus electronic flash, diffusion panels, light placement, and all sorts of things that made my camera-mounted flash seem puny and inadequate. He also told us how he couldn't take pictures of real ice cream because it would melt under the hot lights while he was setting up the shot. Instant mashed potatoes with fake chocolate swirls stood in for the real thing. For the first time I saw light illuminating something that wasn't what it appeared to be. This helped me understand why St. Paul warned his readers that "Satan himself masquerades as an angel of light." Even in the light, all was not quite what we thought it was. Seeing that the light was not always what I thought it was reminded me of a relative of mine who prayed the best public prayers I'd ever heard in church. I envied, in a most un-Christian way, her ability to pray. Filled with "thees" and "thous" and other biblical sounding words, her prayers were almost like hearing angels choiring—except I knew how much her family hated blacks.

It turned out, as another one of Father Bob's trips showed, dark wasn't always what we thought it was, either. This trip took us to the studio of one of his former students in Cincinnati. The studio was on the second story of a weathered, downtown office building in urgent need of urban renewal. We rode up a quaking, old freight elevator. As we stepped off the elevator, a huge, glistening black canvas confronted us. As we walked by this eight-foot tall by ten-foot wide piece, I thought, *Hmmm, I could paint a shiny black wall. Why am I taking art classes?* A few minutes later the artist joined us. He explained that the black wall was a painting of a vintage Cincinnati Reds championship team. I looked, but I couldn't see even the hint of a Redleg. Then he turned on the overhead and side to side track lighting. Out of the depths of the murky black appeared, in full formal pose of the early twentieth century, the Reds from long ago. They were like prehistoric insects captured in black amber. He explained his technique, which, in my awe, I was not able to take in. I was just struck by how light made something invisible visible. Beholding his work also highlighted my own inadequacies as a painter. I was pretty good as a high-schooler. But I knew I'd never do anything like this with paint. I decided to concentrate on photography. My goal was to be the next Ansel Adams—or at least better than the guy who took my high school graduation photo.

That's how I ended up with Jerry Bontrager at Wilmington College. I arrived there in my junior year, after graduating with my two-year degree from Chatfield. Jerry was always pointing out the difference light made to a photographer. Photography is, after all, the art of capturing the light reflected off objects. Now, I thought I pretty much knew all about light. As a sighted person, I could tell the difference between darkness and light. But Jerry helped me see the different kinds of light—and how they made a difference for a photograph. Light determined how the object I was photographing would appear. The further I went in my photography program, the more I discovered about how light works. That light would have an effect in black and white photography was pretty obvious. It was black and white! Dark and light. Then I learned of the various shades of gray, each dependent upon the tone, slant, and intensity of light. Those grays make photographs pop; they bring black and white photographs to life.

Then I began color photography. As a beginner, I assumed that bright sunlight would make the colors more vibrant. Sometimes it did. At other times, as Jerry pointed out, a rainy, cloudy day that would have an amateur photographer packing her camera back in the bag, was perfect for catching the slight variations of color in a violet's petal or a toddler's apple-red cheeks. Both were things that would be lost in bright light. So I began paying attention to, and taking notes on, the characteristics of light: its source, direction, strength, and color. I started considering what effect light would have on the subject I was shooting. I looked for what parts of the picture the light illuminated and what parts it left in shadow— and what sort of mood that tension created.

That's when I began to see that we are surrounded by all sorts of light and that, in the words of Genesis, they are all good.

ILLUMINATING MOMENT

Breathe deeply.

Relax your body and mind.

Think about the following slowly and gently.

Savor each thought.

When was the first time I really noticed light as something more than an absence of darkness?

I also learned to see how the various kinds of light changed how I perceived the barns, old fences, rusted tractors, and people I was photographing. Depending on the angle, strength, hue, and tone, these commonplace objects (if you can call people commonplace) became imbued with a beauty, dignity, and grace that hadn't been obvious unless I Minded the Light. My sight was slowing down. My slower sight showed beauty all around me—a beauty I drank in and that slaked a soulful thirst I didn't realize I'd had. Minding the Light this way became a spiritual exercise.

I confess to having a predisposition to seeing the spiritual in everything around me. That's partly because I have an artistic eye and temperament. But it's also partly because such a predisposition is pretty typical for a Quaker. One of our tenets is that there's something of God in everyone. Another is that all of life is sacramental. Another is that there's redemption everywhere we look—in the down-and-outer asking for loose change and the fading "Visit Rock City" sign on the abandoned, broken-down barn surrounded by waist-high field weeds.

Since God and redemption were all around me, Minding the Light helped me recognize them in a way I hadn't before. I resonated with what the photographer Jan Phillips said: "Every step in the process of taking pictures is a step toward the light, an experience of the holy, an encounter with the God who is at eye level, whose image I see wherever I look." As I began really looking, I, too, saw God everywhere. I even began putting together photo essays for my other classes. While the students in my Bible class turned in ten-page papers on Christology, I gave slide shows. I scored slides of the common life around me to New Testament verses and to the songwriter Mason Williams's "Sunflower." Everywhere I looked I saw evidence of God. Perhaps that's because, as Minor White says, "The ultimate experience of anything is a realization of what's behind it." Like White, I was realizing that God was behind—and in— it all.

As my study of light in photography continued, I found new appreciation for all sorts of light. I was used to sunlight, moonlight, and city lights. These were all lights that I recognized. Then I began to notice that sunlight consisted of infinite qualities—it was not just one thing. Sunlight at 7 AM on a June morning was far different from sunlight at 2 PM that same afternoon. February's sunlight was different from April's or October's. I began making up names and definitions for the light I experienced—fall light, spring light, summer light, winter light. Fall light was golden and warm, with a hint of crispness to it. Summer light was often washed out with haze—I had to use filters to get just the right photograph. Cloud light was a diffused light that settled easily on the eye and on the soul. No stark shadows there— everything was smooth and evenly lit.

In addition to my made-up names for light, I also learned some of its more formal names: direct light (for example sunlight), reflected light (this happens when light from either the sun or sky is bounced off some surface), and alternative light (camera flashes, lightbulbs, car headlights, and many more). I began to think about them spiritually, too. Probably because I had this theological bent, at the same time I was majoring in photography I was minoring in religious studies. So I began to think of direct light as God at work in us, reflected light as God in the people around me, and alternative light as things like the Bible, works of good art, poetry, literature, and more. I was blessed with a wonderful religion professor named T. Canby Jones who encouraged my exercises in spiritual imagination. Canby also introduced me to a little book called *Christian Faith and Practice in the Experience of the Society of Friends.*

Faith and Practice is filled with writings by Quakers through the years. Their pieces address how Friends see faith and how it's practiced as important and as an art. There's even one section entitled "The Art of Living." At the same time that I was learning to see natural light as a means of seeing things in a new way, I also found that there was a spiritual correlation to this new way of seeing. In *Faith and Practice*, I met Caroline Fox of the nineteenth century. She was about the same age as I was during my photography student days when she wrote in her journal of "the struggle through which a spark of true faith was lighted in my soul." Her journal piece also talked about minding the different types of light—"The first gleam of light, 'the first cold light of morning' which gave promise of day with its noontide glories, dawned on me one day. . . . 'Live up to the light thou hast, and more will be granted thee.' Then I believed that God speaks to man by His Spirit. I strove to lead a more Christian life, in unison with what I knew to be right, and looked for brighter days, not forgetting the blessings that are granted to prayer."

Caroline, in her spiritual awakening, began to see the first cold light of morning, noontide glories, and more. While

hers was nineteenth-century language, she helped me see that
all light was indeed God's Light if I learned to see it that way.

ILLUMINATING MOMENT
Breathe deeply.
Relax your body and mind.
Think about the following slowly and gently.
Savor each thought.
*What, for me, would make light more than
something merely natural?*

Seeing the different kinds of light isn't something that just
happens. Deep seeing takes some practice—practice at paying
attention. I'm an old guy, so I tend to dress up at least a
little bit when I'm asked to give a speech or a presentation.
I have one necktie I usually wear when I'm speaking about
paying attention to light, and life, and God. When I walk
into a room wearing that necktie, people look at the tie as a
part of forming a visual expression of this guy who's going
to bore them to tears for the next however long they have
to be there. They glance at the tie and then move on. They
don't pay attention to it. Accustomed to too much visual
stimulation, they often lose the ability to focus on something
and really see it. Sometime during my presentation I'll say
something about how attentiveness to God and God's creation, whether in holding silence or Minding the Light, can be
playful if we pay attention. "That's what my tie represents,"

I say. "Did anybody notice it?" Then people look up. Even from across the room, they try to see the tie and figure out what I mean. What they see is a maroon tie with bits of gold, brown, and blue on it. After the presentation, folks will come up to me. Some slyly try to make conversation while checking out the tie. Others just grab it, lift it close to their face, and begin scrutinizing it.

"Ah, dogs," they'll say and smile. Yes, the tie is filled with all sorts of whimsical dogs.

"That's not all," I reply. Many of them frown, sure they've paid close attention. They squinch their eyes and look some more. Then, usually a small chuckle: "Fire hydrant." Yes, toward the bottom of the tie, in midst of all these doggies, is a tiny pink fire hydrant, placed there by the Savannah College of Art & Design alumna Robbi Behr. Behr, a textile artist and illustrator, has a full line of these quirky ties—full of cheese and one little happy mouse; toilets and one with the seat up; frogs with one catching a fly. They each require that observers pay attention. It's not a paying attention to something that obviously needs paying attention to, such as when you see an M.C. Escher print. Rather, it's that a necktie with dogs is sort of ordinary—so ordinary that we often don't truly see it.

This is probably why Freeman Patterson once said, "If you do not see what is around you every day, what will you see when you go to Tangiers?" How can we ever learn to see the extraordinary if we never learn to see the amazing ordinary? Our eyes, inner and outer, need to be exercised. Musicians know that about their ears. Unless they practice daily, they'll lose their ability to hear tiny differences of tone and note. The same is true if we want to learn how to see attentively. The best way to learn how to see is to practice seeing. It may mean beginning small. Steal a half hour at lunch time and look at the people around you at the restaurant—look at how the light plays across their faces, drapes their clothes, and so on. Don't stare too long, or you might get a chance to observe the food court security guard up close and in a completely new light. Take an hour in the evening to observe how the light changes as it moves across your yard or through your apartment. Pick something around you and check how it looks at different hours of light throughout your weekend.

While you're learning to see the light play, ask yourself, "Where is God playing in this light? Do I see my life in a new way?" Jan Phillips, the photographer I mentioned earlier, says that when she does that, "My eyes find God everywhere, in every living thing, creature, person, in every act of kindness, act of nature, act of Grace. Everywhere I look, there God is, looking back, looking straight back." When she says that, she echoes the eighteenth-century Polish rabbi Menachem Mendel, who said, "Whoever does not see God in every place does not see God in any place."

Don't be discouraged if you don't see straight away with the eye of a Phillips, Patterson, or Mendel. Seeing attentively is a spiritual discipline. As such, it doesn't happen quickly. In fact, one of the joys of spiritual seeing is the slow opening of sight—the noticing of something previously unnoticed. It's finally beholding the brilliance of love ablaze in the world and of seeing Christ at play in ten thousand places. It's the evolving joy of evolving sight.

ILLUMINATING MOMENT
Breathe deeply.
Relax your body and mind.
Think about the following slowly and gently.
Savor each thought.
How might I see God in every place?

My wife, Nancy, has always been a looker. Usually when a man says something like that, he means the woman's attractive. And Nancy is—and always has been—to me. But that's not what I mean. What I mean is that she really looks at things, especially in the world around her. She especially pays attention to light. She loves sunrises (seldom seen by me) and sunsets. She loves to watch the sun work its way across the sky and enjoys how it illuminates the woods and fields around our house. She marks the position of the moon as it moves through the various night skies—winter, spring, summer, fall—by how and where it appears in our great room's two-story window. She's been known to call family members and tell them to go outside and watch the sky for cloud formations, meteor showers, and other atmospheric phenomena. One time, after a particularly stormy day, she saw a double rainbow. She called our son-in-law Mark. "Did you see the rainbows?" she asked. "No, ma'am," he replied, his Scandinavian terse politeness coming across the phone lines. "Well, did you *look?*" she demanded.

Nancy stays up until two AM in mid-November to see the Leonid meteor showers. The Leonids are fast meteors and they leave lots of trains. As they enter earth's atmosphere at speeds of more than 158,000 miles per hour, on a clear, dark night Nancy can see ten or fifteen Leonids in an hour. I won't see any, unless one sails through my bedroom window—something scientific studies assure me is unlikely to happen.

Nancy will occasionally coerce me outdoors to watch the night sky or see a dawn or behold a sunset. And in doing so she has slowly taught me to appreciate those things.

You see, even though I was trained to see with an artistic eye, I used it mostly in that context. I used it to look when I needed to look—with a camera to my eye or a piece of watercolor paper taped to the easel in front of me. In daily life I was able to see the spectacular—the sun setting over the crest of the Collegiate range of the Rockies or rays breaking through storm clouds after a particularly violent thunderstorm or tornado.

Nancy, on the other hand, sees beauty in every noon or moon. She perceives the subtle differences. When we were newlyweds, I rushed to see everything she wanted me to see. I'd stand looking at the sun dipping below the horizon as she extolled the beauty therein. And I'd think, *Um, huh. I love you, kid, but that looks just like last night's sunset. Same time, same channel.* One time I must have said it aloud instead of thinking it. She looked at me. Instead of being upset, she said, "Nope, it's different. Look there. Tonight the low clouds are turning the sky pink here and are tinged with blue on top. Last night the clouds were higher and the sun lit the bottoms and cast the tops in darkness. See?"

I am starting to. Now, when we have visitors to the farm and the sunlight does amazing things, I call them to see the sun set across the corn-stubbled fields, or throw forty-foot-long shadows as we walk, or behold how the setting sun in the west casts a warm, golden light into the woods to our east, lighting the trees in such a way that they seem to cast more light than does the sun.

I still don't care for sunrises much. But Nancy may get me there someday.

Nancy has become my teacher. In a much different way from McLinn or Bontrager or Father Bob or any of my other art teachers, she has taught me to appreciate the everyday light and the lighting of everyday things. There is joy and life in beholding the world around me—trees, deer scampering for cover and casting long shadows across the field, and Nancy herself, face glowing golden, white hair filled with red again as it picks up the colors around us.

I L L U M I N A T I N G   M O M E N T
Breathe deeply.
Relax your body and mind.
Think about the following slowly and gently.
Savor each thought.
Who can be my teacher in the art of seeing?

The first step I learned about Minding the Light around us is to look. This sounds obvious, and probably is. Begin noticing the things around you. Look deeply at them. Look for textures, reflections, tones, and hues. Does the light smooth the thing you're looking at? Or highlight its surface variations? Is what you're looking at absorbing the light? Or reflecting it? Or both—like my denim-clad leg that is half in the sunlight coming through the window and half in the room's shadow? Are the colors muted or bright? What kind of mood does the light create? How does the light do things to the room or the space you're in? My office changes throughout the day as the light moves through it. It's different in winter than summer. I notice some objects in my room more in winter than I do in summer, and vice versa, because the presence and presentation of light changes depending on the season. In summer the light streams through my windows at a higher angle and seems stronger than in winter. In winter, it shoots through at a low angle and feels harsher than in summer. The shadows are more distinct. Perhaps that has something to do with the humidity in Indiana—summers are often humid, and all the moisture in the air diffuses the light. In winter, the humidity drops, and the light seems more crystalline and hard as the temperature goes down.

Look at your light. You can't observe all seasons in a day. Take time to look. Observe your surroundings. Cast your gaze on the furniture, the pictures, the knickknacks, and all the various objects around you. What do you notice? Why does this or that capture your eye?

Learning to see deeply takes time. Most of us, though, don't have lots of time to just look. Our bosses or kids don't want us staring around the room—they want us signing contracts or fixing lunch. Yet, these, too, are opportunities to see light at work—at the boss's face as it turns red from demanding the contracts and the kids' faces as they turn blue from holding their breath waiting for a grilled cheese sandwich.

Seriously, though, grab some moments for intense looking throughout the day. If we are lucky, people and things we love and want to pay attention to already surround us. That means that two of the main ingredients in deep seeing are already present—attention and love. I love the people I work with (though I rarely express it quite that way) and the work I've been given to do. Both the people and the work become life-giving instead of life-draining when I pay attention to them in love. I see each as important and integral to my life. It's not that attention and love make my work or the people any less demanding or time consuming. I'm still busy, going from meeting to meeting and task to task. It's just that carrying some inner sight arising from the attention and love I've paid means that I see God at work. And since that's where I spend most of my time, I need to learn to see God in the people, work, and things around me. While we may not be able to take hours to sit and look around our workspace—whether it's home, office, or factory floor— even the busiest of us can grab quick glimpses of life. Take a half hour at lunchtime to look, and an hour in the evening or before work. And a few hours on a day off.

Start small. Don't try to see everything deeply. Focus on something manageable—not the whole lifescape around you. Some people find this easy to do—to look at one thing and reflect on what it's showing them about life and God. For others, a good way to learn to focus is to buy an inexpensive film or digital camera. Look at the world and what's in it through the tiny viewfinder (not the LCD display that most digital cameras come with). The viewfinder is important because it shows, at a one-step remove (the glass), the world you're trying to see. The LCD gives you an electronic version, but it is many steps removed from the natural world.

This is similar to what you see in the "The Making of . . ." extras tacked on to almost every DVD movie release. In them there is always some clip of the director making a frame with his fingers to get an idea of what the shot will look like on-screen. Or he uses a director's viewfinder—basically a lens without a camera. The point is that the director knows what he wants the audience to see—so he has to narrow his focus and make it fit his mental screen. Using a viewfinder in a camera helps us do the same thing.

It doesn't matter where you go or what you take pictures of. Using a camera forces you to look carefully. The good thing about a digital camera is that you can load the pictures onto your computer and see what you've seen without having to pay for developing and printing costs. Maybe you will take pictures of your office, your dog, or your backyard. Regardless, look at the pictures and ask what the light is doing. Then, tomorrow, at a different time with different light, shoot the same things again and see what they look like.

Look closely at what you see in the pictures. Then write down a list of what you notice—the objects, the people, and the light coming from this direction or that. This task is not easy; it's part of training yourself to see. Take the information and sit with it until the holy ordinary emerges from the clutter into your deepening sight, like a deer track in the jumble of forest litter. What do I know about deer tracks emerging in the jumble of forest litter? I've admitted that I grew up in the city. What I do know is this: Because Nancy and I now live in the country, I often go for walks in the woods. When I first started out, I plunged through the brush and tramped around and came home covered with burrs and with stickers poking through my pants and shirtsleeves. Then I learned to walk along the edge of the woods and look for a place that was mashed down and seemed to lead somewhere. I didn't learn that all on my own—a local forester showed me some tracks while we were figuring out where to plant tree seedlings. Now I spot openings myself. I often find they are deer trails. If I stay on one, other than having to duck under a low-hanging branch, I find that the deer have cleared the way. The way through the forest is open and leads me to some amazing vistas.

Begin small. Notice the difference in the color of the tree limbs in October as opposed to March. In the fall they almost seem to turn black, and in the spring they're bursting with green. And snow is always white—but what kind of white? Grayish-white under a cloudy sky? Bluish-white sprinkled with diamond dust under the sun? My dog, Princess, is white, too. But she looks yellow against the snow and bright white against a green cornfield. There aren't any mistakes. If you take time to separate yourself from everything except the question of seeing, you slowly begin to have your sight skills improved.

I have a feeling that's what the hymn writer Folliot Pierpoint was trying to tell those who sing his words:

For the beauty of the earth
For the glory of the skies,
For the love which from our birth
Over and around us lies.

For the beauty of each hour,
Of the day and of the night,
Hill and vale, and tree and flower,
Sun and moon, and stars of light.

For the joy of ear and eye,
For the heart and mind's delight,
For the mystic harmony
Linking sense to sound and sight.

Lord of all, to Thee we raise,
This our hymn of grateful praise.

Pierpoint wrote this after taking a walk one late spring day in the area near his home in Bath, England. On that walk, Pierpoint saw God in the beauty "of each hour of the day and of the night" and appreciated the "mystic harmony linking sense to sound and sight." He was a person who learned to see deeply. Unfortunately, too often the words of the painter Georgia O'Keeffe reflect my reality more than Pierpoint's do. O'Keeffe said, "Nobody sees a flower really—it is so small it takes time—we haven't time—and to see takes time, like to have a friend takes time." Pierpoint really saw flowers. That made him a friend of God. Taking time to see, even the small things around us, takes us into a friendship available to anyone who wants to really see a flower, a cloud, a person, or God.

ILLUMINATING MOMENT
Breathe deeply.
Relax your body and mind.
Think about the following slowly and gently.
Savor each thought.
How will I practice learning to see?
Will I use a camera?
A pencil or pen, and paper? Or just my imagination?

As you begin to look at the various kinds of lights in your life and how they illuminate your world, begin to list these lights you notice. At first the list may be short—sunlight and moonlight. But, if you begin to pay attention, you'll notice variations or gradations of these—summer sunlight and winter sunlight. Or late summer sunlight and early summer sunlight. Early summer morning, early summer midday, and early summer sunset. Besides naming them, write down your perception of the differences in tone, hue, and intensity. Is the light hard with distinct shadows or soft? How do the different types of light make you feel physically, emotionally, and spiritually? Do some lights bring you closer to God? Why might that be so?

The great photographer Ansel Adams said, "God created light and he divided it into ten zones." Actually, while God created light, it was Adams who defined it by ten zones—a system he developed to help him to control the range of values from light to dark within his photographs. God only knows how many zones there really are—and through Minding the Light, you might come up with some new zones of your own. Light has a soul-filling quality. We cannot truly control light, but we can at least learn how to see by it so that we can behold the divine that surrounds us.

"Every generous act of giving, with every perfect gift, is from above, coming down from the Father of lights," says the writer of the book of James. Every light is a gift from the Father of lights—the plural is very important. The One who gave us life also gave us lights. And sight and sights.

✳
The Light Within
Seeing Ourselves

Ways of Understanding Religion are many. *The Pseudonyms of God*; *The Roaring Stream: A New Zen Reader*; *Faith: Stories: Short Fiction on the Varieties and Vagaries of Faith*; *Searching for God in America*; *Every Eye Beholds You: A World Treasury of Prayer*—these are a few of the titles dealing with spirituality stashed on shelves and piled on tables around our house. Some are from my college and seminary days. Most are nonfiction, but there is a smattering of fiction. Some are Christian. Some are Buddhist. Some are a mixture of the faiths of the world. Some are gifts from friends. Many I bought myself. For all their differences they share one thing—they are each about humanity's search for enlightenment.

One of the blessings of my life is having friends from all flavors of faith. I know rabbis, imams, Christian clergy of all sorts, Buddhists, Hindus, Sikhs, and some other folks about whose religious views I'm not quite sure. From them and from my many books I've learned a fair amount about faiths other than my own particular Christian niche. I know that the spiritual goal of Zen Buddhism is something called "satori." Satori roughly means individual enlightenment as a flash of sudden awareness. In that way it's like the statement we often hear, "It's as if a light went on." Satori is a deep experience of enlightenment attained through personal experience, often by using koans. Koans are riddles, though not like the ones we used to tell in elementary school. "How do you get down off a camel?"—"You don't, you get *down* off a duck." Many koans used today were used by the earliest Zen masters. One of the most famous koans is "What is the sound of one hand clapping?" Daisetz Teitaro Suzuki, one of the twentieth century's leading interpreters of Zen, held that enlightenment was the primary motif of Buddhism and was what set it apart from all other religions.

Islam, too, has its version of enlightenment. Unlike Buddhism, which uses koans that a person ponders in search of enlightenment, Islam begins with its scripture, the Qur'an, to look upward. Enlightenment in Islam involves both the soul and the mind and is rooted in the Qur'an. Everything, from belief to science, is to be seen through the eyes of Islamic faith. That's because, according the Qur'an, "Allah is the Light of the heavens and the earth . . . Light upon light, Allah guideth unto His light whom He will. . . . Allah is Knower of all things."

Hinduism, unlike Buddhism and Islam, teaches that there is no single revelation or established doctrine by which a person achieves enlightenment. Every person has the potential of being enlightened. A Hindu scripture asks:

Who is the Deity we shall worship with our offerings?
It is he who bestows life-force and vigor,
whose guidance all men invoke. . . .

Traditional religious faiths don't hold a monopoly on faith and light. While looking through a listing of newer spirituality concepts, I came across one that was termed "translucence." The originator of this concept, Arjuna Ardagh, says, "I borrowed that word from the physical universe. . . . If you shine light on a translucent object, it appears to glow from within. Translucent people appear to glow from within. A translucent person is someone who has awoken deeply enough to who they really are that their personal agenda of desire and fear become semi-transparent. It's no longer opaque."

While traditional faith seeks enlightenment and contemporary quasi-religion invents new twists on the seeking of light, secular society seeks the light, too. As most of us learned in history class, the eighteenth century saw the rise of an intellectual movement called "The Enlightenment." Some (primarily) European thinkers and writers believed that they were more enlightened than their fellow humans and set out to enlighten them. Notable among them were Immanuel Kant, Jean-Jacques Rousseau, Voltaire, David Hume, John Locke, and America's Thomas Paine. They wanted to fight ignorance, superstition, and tyranny and build a better world. They did so primarily by attacking religion and the aristocracy. In his 1784 essay "What Is Enlightenment?" Kant defined it as follows:

> Enlightenment is man's leaving his self-caused immaturity. Immaturity is the incapacity to use one's own understanding without the guidance of another. Such immaturity is self-caused if its cause is not lack of intelligence, but by lack of determination and courage to use one's intelligence without being guided by another. The motto of enlightenment is therefore: *Sapere aude!* Have courage to use your own intelligence!

Though the writer of Ecclesiastes said, "There is nothing new under the sun," humans do try to come up with new ways, both religious and secular, to find enlightenment. That's why if you search the Internet, you'll come across statements such as "Spiritual enlightenment and spiritual awakening is the primary goal of almost all spiritual practices, traditions, and religions and for any spiritual seeker," and phrases such as "true spiritual enlightenment" and "the endless search for spiritual enlightenment" and "how spiritual enlightenment is the cure for the many problems in society." Beliefnet, the site of all things spiritual, even has "Test Your Enlightenment IQ." This test opens by saying, "From a Buddhist standpoint, there's more to Nirvana than a defunct band from Seattle. See how much you know about the state of deathless peace and bliss." All of these point to the hunger for spiritual light and understanding. Maybe the great Irish theologian Van Morrison is right when he croons, "Enlightenment, don't know what it is."

ILLUMINATING MOMENT
Breathe deeply.
Relax your body and mind.
Think about the following slowly and gently.
Savor each thought.
What spiritual practices do I know that emphasize light?

Unlike Buddhism, Hinduism, and even the concept of translucence, Judaism and Christianity think of spiritual enlightenment as divine illumination. According to my rabbi friend Aaron, the word for light in Hebrew is *or*. *Or* is commonly used as a metaphor for the divine energy that sustains the universe. For Judaism, enlightenment comes from knowledge about this divine energy. That is why Jewish spirituality is grounded in the study of Torah. Midrash and rabbinic interpretation developed to help people understand Torah. Rabbinic teaching says that to be enlightened is the result of spiritual discipline that includes prayer, study, and good works. There's a line from the Mishnah in a section called *Pirke Avoth* (Ethics of the Fathers) that reads, "The world is sustained by three things—*Torah* (study), *Avodah* (prayer) and *Gemilut Hasadim* (acts of loving kindness)."

Study, prayer, and acts of loving kindness also connect with the Christian understanding of enlightenment, though many times the emphasis seems to be placed more on one or two of these things rather than all three together. *Gemilut Hasadim*, though he would not have called it that, was the focus for the seventeenth-century Carmelite monastic

Brother Lawrence. Brother Lawrence described seeing spiritually as "practicing the presence" of God. This is why one of his followers, Joseph de Beaufort, wrote, "Knowing only that God was present, he [Brother Lawrence] walked in the light of faith and was content just to lose himself in God's love no matter what happened." Brother Lawrence believed that acts of loving kindness, performed as offerings to God, give a person sufficient light for learning how to live.

In the twentieth century Agnes Sanford practiced *Avodah*. The daughter of a Presbyterian missionary to China, the wife of an Episcopal rector, and a woman who used Orthodox and other spiritual practices, Sanford brought much illumination to the subject of spiritual light primarily through her understanding of prayer. Her first book, *The Healing Light*, published in 1947, has sold over half a million copies. In it she tells of a time of enlightenment when a minister came to pray for her baby, who was a year and a half old and suffering from an ear infection.

> This incident turned on the light for me in the world that had grown very dark with futility. It showed me that God is an active and powerful reality. True, I understood very little about Him. I merely thought that the visiting minister had the gift of healing. Now I know that he had no gift except that which is open to all of us, the infinite gift of the life of God Himself. . . . God is both within us and without us. He is the source of all life; the creator of universe behind universe; and of unimaginable depths of inter-stellar space and of light-years without end.

But He is also the indwelling life of our own little selves. And just as a whole world full of electricity will not light a house unless the house itself is prepared to receive that electricity, so the infinite and eternal life of God cannot help us unless we are prepared to receive that life within ourselves. . . . "The kingdom of God is within you," said Jesus. And it is the indwelling light, the secret place of the consciousness of the Most High that is the kingdom of Heaven in its present manifestation on this earth. Learning to live in the kingdom of Heaven is learning to turn on the light of God within.

Today there's an emerging Christian practice modeled after the Way of the Cross (*Via Crucis*). It is called the Way of Light (*Via Lucis*) or Stations of the Resurrection. In the same way that the Way of the Cross follows the course of Jesus' passion, death, and burial, The Way of Light celebrates the fifty days from Easter to Pentecost. Though a fairly new practice, the Way of Light was inspired by an ancient inscription from St. Paul's first letter to the church at Corinth, found on a wall of the San Callisto Catacombs on the Appian Way in Rome.

Better known in parts of Western Europe, the Way of Light is gaining ground in the United States, thanks to the spread of books about it. Most popular is *Stations of the Light: Renewing the Ancient Christian Practice of the Via Lucis as a Spiritual Tool for Today* by Mary Ford-Grabowsky. While the Way of Light is not quite as ancient as Ford-Grabowsky implies, she's right to say: "The Way of

Light is a spirituality of joy . . . [where] each exercise seeks to be exhilarating by reinforcing the clear New Testament teaching that spiritual life is an invitation to maximize joy despite deep pain. Saint Anselm of Canterbury said it well some ten centuries ago: 'I have known a joy that is *full*, and *more* than full,' meaning that the depth and breadth of joy that we receive in the spiritual journey surpasses even our greatest expectations."

The Way of Light emphasizes the constant presence of the risen Christ and seeks his guidance and leadership for everything that faces us in daily life. In the same way that walking a labyrinth represents a journey to our personal center and then back out into the world, walking the *Via Lucis* helps us see ourselves as light bearers in a darkened world. Walking the Way of Light is geared toward helping the walker identify with the Lord who always walks ahead, behind, and all around us as we move through our lives.

All of this spiritual emphasis on light is not surprising, especially considering that there are more than 200 verses in the Bible that mention light. Add to that the references to "see" (802 verses) and "sight" (290 verses), and it's easy to see that light and sight are essential parts of Christian faith.

ILLUMINATING MOMENT
Breathe deeply.
Relax your body and mind.
Think about the following slowly and gently.
Savor each thought.
What would a way of light look like for me?

What sets the Quaker understanding of Minding the Light apart from other forms of spiritual enlightenment (which often seem to have something to do with a light going on) is that it implies paying attention to something that's already present. Quakers believe the Light of Christ already shines in each of us. The Inner Light metaphor reminds us that Christ is at work in every one of us. God's Light is there— we just need to learn to heed it.

The early Quakers, particularly, felt that heeding the work of the Light within would give the earnest spiritual seeker "openings" and "leadings." Some openings are simple, yet profound—such as George Fox's when, alone and despairing of all outward advice, he stilled himself, looked within, and heard a voice that told him, "There is one, even Christ Jesus, that can speak to thy condition." When he heard that, he wrote, "my heart did leap for joy." Another early Quaker, James Nayler, had an opening that showed him this:

> There is a spirit which I feel that delights to do no evil, nor to revenge any wrong, but delights to endure all things, in hope to enjoy its own in the end. Its hope is to outlive all wrath and contention, and to weary out all exaltation and cruelty, . . . It sees to the end of all temptations. As it bears no evil in itself, so it conceives none in thoughts to any other. If it be betrayed, it bears it, for its ground and spring is the mercies and forgiveness of God. Its crown is meekness, its life is everlasting love unfeigned.

Openings continue today, giving us new insight into the nature of God and the movement of the Spirit in our lives. They are openings in the same way that when we open the drapes in the morning, we are flooded with light that shows us our surroundings and illuminates our lives. The only difference is that, in the case of the Inner Light, it is our lives that are illuminated, not just our living rooms.

Leadings are often calls to some sort of action. Some early Quakers discerned leadings that told them to pay a visit to the sultan of Turkey (uninvited) or to set sail across the ocean on a specific ship at a specific time to speak to a specific person or group. In my own life, leadings have been a bit less dramatic than that. Still, they have led me to do things I wouldn't necessarily have come up with on my own. I landed at George H.W. Bush International Airport in Houston the night the second Iraq War started. The next evening, like almost another one hundred Quakers, I felt led to demonstrate on behalf of peace. I marched, in my freshly ironed khakis, penny loafers, and button-down shirt, the few blocks to the airport's entrance and held a sign that said, "War is not the answer." I didn't do this because I wanted to make a political statement. I did it because I firmly believe that the gospel of Jesus calls us to stand on the side of peace, not war. I felt called to witness for peace. So, when some cars and trucks stopped and the people inside yelled, cursed, or questioned my patriotism, I stood quiet, peaceful. I was a bit nervous, so, true to my faith, I quaked. But I didn't answer back. I didn't argue. I didn't try to persuade them that I was right. Instead I tried to smile as I prayed for the Light within me, within them, and within the people flying over and in Iraq. We were all linked by the Light, even if we did not recognize or acknowledge it.

Leadings help us see ways to act. If we pay attention to that soul work going on, then we can learn God's will and direction for us. That leads to walking in the Light of the One "who formed our inward parts," ensured that we were "fearfully and wonderfully made," and wrote in his book "all the days that were formed for us, when none of them as yet existed."

While this idea of the Inner Light as a bit of the divine spark placed deep in our hearts sounds as if it could be just some goofy doctrinal quirk of Quakers, it is grounded in the Bible. John's Gospel speaks of Jesus as "The true light, which enlightens everyone" (man, woman and child). It is through this Light of Christ, that God exists among us and knows us each personally. The psalmist says:

> O LORD, you have searched me and known me.
> You know when I sit down and when I rise up;
> you discern my thoughts from far away.
> You search out my path and my lying down,
> and are acquainted with all my ways.
> Even before a word is on my tongue,
> O LORD, you know it completely.
> You hem me in, behind and before,
> and lay your hand upon me.
> Such knowledge is too wonderful for me;
> it is so high that I cannot attain it.

God is within us, God knows us, and that is something, on days good or bad, we can never completely understand. "Such knowledge is too wonderful for me; it is so high that I cannot attain it." To believe that God's Light is within us asks us, as the Southern writer Flannery O'Connor once said, to have "the kind of mind that is willing to have its sense of mystery deepened by contact with reality, and its sense of reality deepened by contact with mystery." That mystery is, for Quakers, the mystery of the Light Within.

Now before you begin to think that this sounds a little too "woo-woo"y, as one of my friends says when she thinks something's spiritually spacey, think about it this way: We all carry traits inherited from our parents, grandparents, great-grandparents . . . Adam and Eve . . . okay, you get the idea. Every one of us has experienced times when we've looked at someone and seen their relatives in them. I know people who knew my father-in-law who see him in my wife. Nancy is as different in personality and physical build as can be from her father. Jim was a bluff, brusque, barrel-chested, round-faced fellow. Nancy is a sweet (most of the time), petite, pretty woman. But she carries her father inside her. Nancy's a great person to attend masquerade parties with—her costumes are rarely elaborate, but they always transform her into someone even I barely recognize. She told me about a time that she dressed up and went to a party where nobody seemed to know who she was. Then a woman looked at her and said, "Hello, Nancy." How did she know? "You've got your father's eyes," she replied. And she does. The same color, shape, and occasional flash of laughter or anger. You can see Jim in Nancy.

Does that mean that Nancy and Jim are the same? No. They are self-differentiated people. But this spark of similarity helps us understand how, as children of God, we have a piece of the Light of God within us, as companion, teacher, friend, and guide. No, we are not God, but there is something of God in us. And this Light goes with us and calls us to remember the One who loves us and in whose image we are each made.

ILLUMINATING MOMENT
Breathe deeply.
Relax your body and mind.
Think about the following slowly and gently.
Savor each thought.
When have I ever had a sense of divine Light within me?

The Inner Light is more than something we merely study. Minding the Light moves us into the realm of experience. Quakers call this kind of living "experiential." By that we mean living the life of the Spirit with soul knowledge and not just head learning. While the words and practices of a particular faith tradition are often helpful to us, we each find ways of learning more about God for ourselves. I carry a variety of things in my spiritual toolbox that help me learn more about God. These change from time to time, depending on the circumstance and where I am in my life and geography. As I'm writing these words, I'm on a retreat in Minnesota, staying in a small apartment overlooking a small lake at St. John's University. I flew here, which meant that I took only those few things that I could cram into my suitcase and briefcase. On the desk next to me is the Catholic *Shorter Christian Prayer*, a four-week Psalter of the liturgy with morning and evening prayers. In the bedroom on the nightstand rests my worn copy of *Quaker Faith and Practice*, a collection of writings about Quaker doctrine and discipline. Out in the rental car is a CD by Beth Neilson Chapman called "Hymns." At noon, even though I'm a Quaker, I'll be going to prayers in St. John's Abbey with the monks.

All of these are helpful to my spiritual condition, but only if I Mind the Light within—only if I let God's working in me come alive and show me how these books, CDs, and worship services can lead me closer to God and to the self I'd like to be, the person I feel God wants me to be and created me for. The Inner Light is, as the apostle Paul says, "Christ in you, the hope of glory." I do find glory in the man I occasionally see myself become when I've paid enough attention to the Inner Light—the human who's calmer, kinder, happier, and more joyful than I often am as I scurry through life. minding the Light offers us a glimpse of the people that, with God's help, we can be. It's sort of like what happens in the film *As Good As It Gets,* mentioned earlier. Melvin, when he sees how he's different when he's around Carol, tells her, "You make me want to be a better man." The Inner Light makes us want to be a better man or woman. That's because it shows us the selves God intended for us to be—those times when we're kinder, gentler, happier, and more gracious than usual and think to ourselves, *Why am I not like that more of the time?*

It's not a self-made glory. It's not something we've done ourselves. It is God's Spirit at work in us. When we see ourselves in the Light, we see ourselves as God sees us. Meister Eckhart said it well when he wrote, "The eye with which I see God is the same as that with which God sees me. My eye and the eye of God are one eye, one vision, one knowledge, and one love. My eye and the eye of God are one."

Minding the Light this way leads me into a fuller revelation of the divine direction than I usually experience. When I Mind the Light, I draw near to God and God draws near to me. The distance between my day-to-day world and my inner life begins to close. This nearness to God teaches me to be led by the Light God gives me. It also teaches me to trust that God has given me all the Light I need for this time in my life. That last part is hard for me. I'm willing to be led –I just want searchlights instead of flashlights lighting the way. Slowly, God is showing me how, sometimes, more light is too much light. One December evening I battled my way home through a snowstorm. My normal twenty-minute commute took two hours. The glare of oncoming headlights mixed with the fast, falling snow. Turning onto our country road, I found that mine was the only car. It was hard to see—no streetlamps out here. I had a hard time telling where the snow-covered road ended and the snow-covered ditch began. I thought I needed more light—so I flipped my high beams on. Mistake. The reflected light from the thick snow blinded me. I quickly dimmed them and made my way slowly home by the light I had. It was enough.

For snowstorms or interior storms in our lives, more light, especially divine brilliance, may be too much. When Moses came down off Mount Sinai, his face shone with the brilliance of having been with God. But the glory was too much for the people. "When Aaron and all the Israelites saw Moses, the skin of his face was shining, and they were afraid to come near him." Too much Divine Light may overpower and frighten us. So God gives us the amount of Light that we can handle and enough to light our way.

When we learn to live with the Light we've been given, life becomes a quietly satisfying journey. Because even though the light is gentle, it takes us, as Mary Blackmar says, to a ". . . growing frame of wisdom, 'shining more and more unto the perfect day.'" It may be barely enough light to see by, but it is enough to be *seen* by.

There are times that the Inner Light is like a small, flickering candle. My friend Sue often lights candles for people and situations she's praying for. The candles are a part of her Catholic tradition that I appreciate. She showed me a website that the Carmelites of Indianapolis have. You can light a virtual candle there and send a prayer request to the sisters. Though Quakers don't light candles, except for romantic dinners, I occasionally go and light an e-candle for Sue and some issue or concern she's facing. Usually, though, it's she who has lit the candle for me. Sometimes, just knowing that my friend has lit a candle for me—a small, flickering token of love and prayer—is all I need. I sense God's presence because a little light to guide me was all I needed.

The Inner Light can be like that—a gentle godly reminder that we are not alone in this journey. That God is ever-present. That where we walk, so, too, does God walk.

ILLUMINATING MOMENT
Breathe deeply.
Relax your body and mind.
Think about the following slowly and gently.
Savor each thought.
When have I felt God to be like candlelight—
a light of constant presence?

For me, the image of the Inner Light as a flickering candle is a comforting one. But my Quaker tradition also has an image of the Inner Light that is much less comfortable. That's an idea of the Inner Light as spiritual spotlight, showing us the sides of ourselves we'd rather not see, the sides that are not kinder, gentler, happier, and more gracious.

When I think of that depiction, I remember the prison spotlight in the movies I used to love as a kid. My favorites were when a James Cagney sort of guy planned a jailbreak. Obviously guilty and headed for the electric chair or the gas chamber, he'd plot and plan and make a break for it. Just before he got across the prison yard or through a gap in barbed wire atop the wall, the prison sirens wailed, their piercing sound eerily rising and falling. Searchlights popped on and tracked across the yard and up the walls until the tiny silhouette was spotted—black as sin against the pure white of light. A look of horror crossed the baddie's face; his doom was sealed. A bad man was about to be brought low. Then the machine guns started to stutter stitch their way to and through him. A gangster whose sins had found him out.

As a pacifistic Quaker I wasn't supposed to enjoy all this violence, but I did. And in those black and white movie days, crime didn't pay, except in the biblical sense—the wages of sin was death. Even though my theology and understanding of God are a bit deeper than when I was a preteen lying on the dining room floor watching a humming television set the size of a small refrigerator, there's part of those prison movies that is still true in the Quaker understanding of the Inner Light. That's the searchlight part. That's the not-so-easy part of wanting to know God.

I know I have a *film noir* gangster inside me. Do I need to worry that God will be like the warden in the prison movies, turn a spotlight on me to search out my sin, and then gun me down? After all, John's first letter tells us, "This is the message we have heard from him and proclaim to you, that God is light and in him is no darkness at all." How can I get close to God if I have darkness in my life?

Unlike the movie searchlight that searches so the baddie can be punished, God's inner searchlight searches so I can see myself honestly. In the glaring Light of the Spirit, honesty is the only option. I see myself as I am and want to throw myself on the mercy of the Lord's court. When I was a young minister I helped officiate at my grandfather's funeral. By the time it was over I was a wreck—emotional, feeling the loss, hoping I hadn't said something stupid, and so on. I shouldn't have tried to drive, distracted as I was. But I did. As we got back to my grandparents' house for the after-funeral meal, a car tailgated me down the narrow one-way street they lived on, making me edgier than I already was. I sped up past the twenty-five mph posted speed. When I spotted a parking place in front of my grandparents' house, instead of going slightly past it, stopping, and then backing in to parallel park, I tried pulling into the slot. I was more than halfway in when I heard metal on metal, screeching down the side of the car. I had torn a gash in my back passenger door and fender. Worse, I'd ripped the bumper off the brand-new truck that I'd tried to squeeze in front of.

I knew most of my grandparents' neighbors—and their cars. But I didn't recognize that truck. I didn't know who to apologize to. I waited for my folks to get there. Surely Dad would know whose truck it was. He did. He saw what happened, shook his head, and said, "It's none of the neighbors', son. It's your Uncle Lew's."

For many people, this might sound like a good thing, since it was a family member's vehicle. But my dad's older brother, Lewis J. Bill, Jr., was the epitome of the Ohio State Highway patrolman—tall, stern, no-nonsense. This guy had arrested his own wife for speeding. I had wrecked his new truck. On the day of his father's funeral. The funeral at which I'd probably said something that sounded like "blah, blah, blah, blah, . . . I'm an idiot." The funeral of the man he'd been named for.

I dreaded standing before him. Next to his pure highway patrolman morality, I was a sinner of the first degree. Speeding. Causing a wreck. Failing to report an accident. I could picture him coming up with a list—it was so easy for me that I knew he'd come up with even more.

The limousine dropped my grandmother and Uncle Lew off. He saw his truck, bumper askew. I walked trembling toward him, twenty-four years old, feeling ten. "I wrecked your truck." I stammered out the whole sordid story. His stony face was set. I waited for a storm to break. Instead, he opened his arms, wrapped my 5'7" frame in his 6'2" one, and said, "That hardly seems to matter today, does it? Thanks for what you said about Dad." A tear ran down his cheek.

That's what that inner searchlight does for us. Yes, it can be painful; pointing out things we'd rather not see or admit. At the same time, Minding the Light leads us into a place where we can admit what needs to be admitted and then into a place of acceptance and forgiveness. The light helps us see what we need to see, so that that which is wrong or harmful can be washed away in the clear Light of God's love. As the first Friend, George Fox, said, "The light that shows us our sins is the light that takes them away."

Fox also said that he saw "that there was an ocean of darkness." The searching Inner Light makes it seem that way in our world and our personal lives at times. But Fox goes on to say that he also saw "an infinite ocean of light and love, which flowed over the ocean of darkness. In that also I saw the infinite love of God." We place our darkness into the infinite loving Light of God and leave it there—trusting that Light and Love to heal us.

ILLUMINATING MOMENT
Breathe deeply.
Relax your body and mind.
Think about the following slowly and gently.
Savor each thought.
Have I ever felt God's Light like a searchlight—
harsh and pointing out things I'd just as soon not see?
Did that Light leave me in a place of discomfort?

Minding the Light leads us to a place where we're not drifting upon a sea of uncertainty. We are called to trust. Garrett Keizer writes in *A Dresser of Sycamore Trees*:

> All of us are like passengers strapped into the wildest ride at the amusement park, who suddenly recognize as the gears begin to whine and the faces of the other riders blur that only a few screws and bearings stand between themselves and death, that people can die, do die, on rides just like this one, and you can't get off simply by wishing you hadn't gotten on. The only decision one really has then is to believe or not to believe that the apparatus and its operator are trustworthy.

That's hard on the dark days when the car is clanking up the steep slope, drawn by the unseen lift chain over which we have no control, and it looks as if we'll rocket toward doom on the down slope. But depending on God's Light—

even as we're about to careen over the edge—teaches us that life is an adventure with a trustworthy guide.

I used to take high school kids to Colorado for summer camp. One part of our trip was climbing Mt. Princeton. I'd tell the kids that they were in for an adventure. "Great," they'd reply, "we're going to have some fun." "That's not what I said," I'd reply. "I said it was going to be an adventure. But it won't always be fun." And it wasn't. The mountain trails were steep. Sometimes we'd get caught in snowstorms at the summit—even in July or August. Then there'd be the usual late-afternoon thunderstorms. The rocky trails became slick and the footing less than sure. The kids soon found that it required concentration, caution, teamwork, and a knowledgeable guide to climb successfully up and down the mountainside. It was not at all like hiking the rolling, grass-covered hills of central Ohio.

While living through this adventure, some kids whined about how hard it was, or how scared or wet they were, and on and on. At first, smiles and laughter lit the way—until the rough times hit. "I'm never going to do this again," they'd moan, "this is awful."

When the climb was over and we'd arrived where the buses waited to take us back to camp and to dry clothes, the whining began tapering off. By the time the dinner bell rang, and the kids were showered and clean and dry, they were chattering about the climb and relishing the bond they had formed in the adventure while placing their safety in the hands of others.

The Light holds us safe. Ultimately. We are vouchsafed only at the end of the journey. Along that way, as the Light guides, it can also heal. Nancy had a particularly difficult time with a person who she felt was taking financial and other advantages of Nancy's dying father. This simmered inside her for years. It bothered her. She says that her bitterness was working a brew inside her that was poisoning her. So during those years, being the person of faith she is, she allowed God's loving Light to work on her. One day she announced to me, "I've let it go. I don't hate 'Madame X' anymore. I don't know her well enough to hate her and no one deserves to be hated. I hate what she's done to my dad and our family, but it's time to let it go."

Now, these two did not become fast friends. Nor did this feeling deter Nancy in her efforts to protect her father's assets and the family's legacy. But now it was done without a bitterness that sapped the love and light out of Nancy. The loving Light of God shone in her and then through her and healed an open emotional wound. As she quit thinking hatefully about this woman, she quit speaking hatefully, too. So did I. So did her brothers and sister. Not right away. The healing took time. It's still continuing. Doing so doesn't deny the pain or that there's scarring. But now we're moving ahead with our lives instead of constantly looking back on the damage done.

ILLUMINATING MOMENT

Breathe deeply.

Relax your body and mind.

Think about the following slowly and gently.

Savor each thought.

When have I felt God's healing Light?

How would I describe it?

A friend of mine, Mary Brown, is a poet. Cinquains, clerihews, quatrains, odes, sestinas and sonnets—poetic forms of all types are her forte. I know little about poetry (as Mary will attest), but I do know what I like. I clip poems from magazines. I buy books of poems—from Walt Whitman to e.e. cummings to Wendell Berry and more. I even have a book of parody poetry (*The Brand X Anthology of Poetry*). When Mary sent me "Early Spring Aubade," I didn't know that an aubade was a poem or song of or about lovers separating at dawn, but I did know that her poem reminded me that light is a quivering grace that makes me seek God's help in being a better man. That man is one that hungers for goodness, beauty, love, and a very real connection with the Great Lover of my soul from whom I separate too often.

> The branches outside this office window
> too often block the light, but today the early
>
> morning sun wavers, then prevails, stippling
> this space with a tentative dawn that crawls
>
> toward an even more fragile day. All the failures
> of my life on earth are erased in this quivering
>
> grace that works its lacy way through its own
> curious birth. This is the one appointed hour
>
> that comes and gives and goes again—too soon—
> the briefest visit, that leaves this faltering glow,

the gift of a faint, definite urging, the finest
power we have—so close, this close, to Love.

This gift of a faint, but definite urging toward the finest
power I have reminds me that God loves me. This love is
often revealed only by light.

CHAPTER FOUR

✳

The Light Without
Seeing Others

A smiling fox greets meet me every morning when I arrive at my office. Unlike the very real and furry yipping coyotes that wake me on the farm, this cheerful chap is a cartoon. A whimsical red fox with a big smile and dressed in seventeenth-century coat and hat, he swings a lantern while walking down a country lane. Beneath him are some words of George Fox—". . . walk cheerfully over the world, answering that of God in everyone." I keep that poster right across from my desk. It reminds me to look for God in every person who comes into that room—whether it's someone coming to the Indianapolis Center for Congregations for assistance or a fellow staff member who's asking for another vacation day. George the Fox's jaunty step helps me remember that seeing God in every person is something that brings me joy, along with a smile to my soul that may work its way out to my face if I let it.

I often forget to look for God in everyone. Seeing God in others is easier when I'm with my friends—they're as witty and charming as I am! Our differences don't seem to matter.

I call Aaron, who works in the office next to mine, my little brother, both because he's younger than me and because he's shorter. But I call him brother mostly because we grew up in the same city, love British sports cars, quirky humor, Ohio State football, music, and more. We have a lot in common. But we have major differences—I'm older and Quaker; he's younger and Jewish. Thanks to my friendship with Aaron, though, these differences have enriched my life. I've had the chance to experience Seder meals at his home, attend a Bat Mitzvah, become better friends with rabbis in town (two of whom are writers like me!), and make new friends. My life is blessed because Aaron and his difference from me are a part of my life. I look at him and it's easy to see God in him—he's kind, loving, smart, and, well, I don't want to say too many nice things about him because he'll probably read this book and then become insufferable. Still because of my seeing that of God in him—and hopefully his seeing that of God in me—we have come to depend on one another. We watch our differences develop into things we treasure about each other.

When I see God shining in the facial expressions, comments, and body language of the people I see every day, I appreciate things that could separate us—age, sex, physique, race, and culture. Such seeing doesn't deny the differences, but it helps me perceive them as gifts. This then leads me further down the path where there's a possibility of my learning to love them in the same way God loves them and me.

I recently came across a Jewish prayer that reminds me to do just that. *Baruch atah Adonai elohaynu melech ha'olam mishaneh ha'briyot*—"Blessed art thou, Lord our God, King of the Universe, who dost vary the aspect of thy creatures." The note above it says that it's to be prayed upon "seeing a person of abnormal appearance." There are days I think everyone else is a person of abnormal appearance. One of the joys, though, of working downtown is seeing the variety of people who come there. Some, for physical or emotional reasons, are of abnormal appearance. There are times I'd rather not be bothered by them, but then I am hit with twinges of guilt—a positive residual effect of an upbringing long on Bible memorization. I remember Jesus' words, "Truly I tell you, just as you did it to one of the least of these who are members of my family, you did it to me." Some of the folks I see are the least of these, at least by the gentrified standards of most of the folks I see in restaurants and offices around mine. But Jesus says they are "members of my family," and this leads me to see God in them. At times it has meant I've stopped and spoken to the babbling man wanting to receive a handout and to be given a ride, my middle-class knees knocking all the way, and to the kid whose car died in the grocery store parking lot.

Sometimes the least of these are the most of these. The very wealthy or powerful are different from me, too. They're persons of abnormal appearance in another way. And sometimes I find it more difficult to be charitable to these "ins" than to the "outs." Especially when they're of a different political persuasion than I. But God's family tree grows in them as surely as it does in anybody. I need to pray and care for them, too. Sometimes it's our differences that lead me to see God in them. Our differences, not our similarities, can lead us to a new way of seeing God. Such sight helps me keep from creating God in my own image. It expands my spiritual vistas.

Seeing that of God in the poor and the rich and the people like me is easiest when they're pleasant. But seeing God in others is lots harder if I find the others annoying. Like the night Nancy invited a guest for dinner. When I heard he was coming, I groaned inwardly. I must have groaned outwardly, too, because Nancy said, "Oh, and his coming is a bad thing?" No, it's not a bad thing. It's just that, at that time in my life, I found him sort of annoying. For one, he thinks he knows everything. (Of course, I *do* know everything!) He fractures words and phrases (he uses a "digical" camera). I love words used well. He talks constantly. ". . . and then I told her that, oh, is that ice cream? We used to make the best ice cream. Oh, that. . . " That means I don't get to say anything. (You've probably noticed that my annoyance was more about me than about him.)

Nancy invited him because he was a long way from his home and had been for while. He was also someone she loves. So I decided to try and see him through her eyes that evening. Doing so also reminded me to try seeing him through God's eyes.

We sat down to supper, and over the meal I heard some words that fit no pronunciation keys in any dictionary of any known language. I tried not to grimace, but my eyes gave me away. "I get my words mixed up sometimes when I talk," he laughed. "When it comes to words, I'm just a bull in a Chinese shop." I found that his mix-ups with language were engaging—the "bull in a Chinese shop" is so delightful, close but not quite right—that I became more playful with language as well. Okay, the evening didn't end with him as my new best friend. Or even second-best friend. But I did come to a new appreciation of him that evening. Perhaps that's because, as the Spanish Jesuit philosopher and writer Baltasar Gracián said, "When the eyes see what they have never seen before, the heart feels what it has never felt."

Seeing what I'd not seen before helped me enjoy that evening with Nancy's older brother and engendered new feelings of kinship toward him myself. This good-hearted fellow's talk about his wife, kids, and love of the Indiana landscape reminded me of my own feelings about those things in my life. I remembered how he'd helped me and my dad chainsaw fallen trees while Nancy and I were building our house. He's not afraid of hard work. Sitting with him that evening in the fading light, pie on our plates and coffee in our cups, my heart, filled with gratitude and humilty, felt what it had never before felt.

ILLUMINATING MOMENT
Breathe deeply.
Relax your body and mind.
Think about the following slowly and gently.
Savor each thought.
What would it feel like to try to see someone as God sees him or her?

Linus Van Pelt, the famous blanket-dragging philosopher of *Peanuts* fame, once declaimed to his sister Lucy that he was going to be a doctor and help the world. She pointed out how he had difficulty relating to people. To which he exclaimed, "I love mankind; it's people I can't stand." I know how he feels. It's easy for me to believe that everyone on this planet is God's child. I just have a hard time loving them when they're the yahoo who took the last loaf of fresh-baked bread in the grocery. Seeing God in others is easy in my head. It's a little harder when the yeasty aroma's wafting to me in the checkout line.

Linus's sentiment rings true with many of us. Yes, I can love every homeless child, every neighbor, every criminal, every fellow worker, even every television preacher and used-car salesman in the abstract. It's when they are up close, and I perceive them as stinky, lying, cheating, wanting something, and personal that I have a problem. It's not that the light isn't shining in them—it's just that I haven't looked at them through the eyes of God's love so I can see it.

Thomas Jeavons, the lead staff person for the Philadelphia Yearly Meeting of Friends, wrote this about the concept of seeing that of God in every person:

> As statements of core beliefs go, this is a good one: catchy, fairly simple, even biblically sound (see John 1:9). . . . However, this . . . is an invitation to a faith which, while it promises a great deal for us, also requires a great deal of us. To say there is that of God in each of us, or we are each given a measure of the Divine light, is to speak about our potential. This truth reminds us of one reason we should treat every person with dignity and respect . . . [and]

reminds us we are talking about the possibilities
with which God imbues our lives, and the challenges.

"The possibilities and challenges with which God imbues
our lives." And other people's lives: How do I even start seeing
God's Light in them? For me it begins by seeing what we
might have in common. The fellow that grabbed the last
loaf of bread with its freshly baked aroma is standing in
front of me, smiling at his young son. The young woman
who cut me off on the freeway could be my daughter as
surely as she is someone else's. Jeanne Murray Walker
helped me see the Light of God in that young woman
through her poem, "Little blessing spoken in road rage":

> Chariot from Hades, fire
> glinting from its windshield, steel
> knife splitting the atom
> to pull in front of me,
> so close now I can see
> the driver, her phone, can hear
> death ring. Searching
> for a place to get away, I swerve
> into a corridor of hate,
> detesting her, my body fired
> with full throttle hatred,
> I rev up, speed ahead, so
> close now I can see her
> her mouth a frightened grimace.
> How exposed she is, wearing
> only the flimsy dress of a car,

her brief thee etched
and dying on the air, when
someone calls, Bless this
child. May her parents see
her alive tonight, speaking
through me, a voice, then
peace, as she passes safely by.

When I learn to see others by God's Light, I find that their oddities and unusual traits are probably not so different from my own. Beholding them this way doesn't let me remain untouched by their lives. I cross paths all day long with people filled with joys and sorrows, hopes and fears. When I take time to see the traces of God in and through them—the compassionate smile, the delight in a child's achievement, the ten-dollar bill surreptitiously skipped into the outstretched cup—I see things that cement our fragile bond of divine family.

Douglas Steere, a great witness to the life of the spirit, once wrote,

> I hold up persons before God in intercession, loving and seeing them under God's eyes, longing for God's healing and redeeming power to course through their lives. I hold up certain social situations, certain projects. At such a time I often see things that I may do in company with or that are related to this person or to this situation. I hold up the persons . . . and their needs, as I know them, to God.

I can't pray for someone and not begin to feel the bond between us of God's family ties. That is, if I'm praying something deeper than, "Please, God, make that person not such a jerk," or "Open their eyes to see things my way, Lord."

I have to begin where I sense a need in their lives, even if it's a simple one. Many years ago I read a little piece that helped me a lot—it described prayer as *passionate thinking*. Now I'm not a very good formal pray-er—I don't do well at closing my eyes and reciting prayers. I've always found it hard to set a regular time each day to pray. But I can think passionately about people and their lives. So I do. I begin by imagining them wrapped in God's loving Light. That's how I pray—maybe something like that will work for you.

An immediate prayer for someone else moves me outside myself to seeing them with God's loving eyes. I don't have to know more than that there was sadness in their eyes. That's enough. I don't have to run down the hall and embrace them and invite them to pour out their heart. At my office, I might just find that they were sad because the copy machine jammed or it's out of toner.

When this really gets difficult is when we're thinking about somebody we have a conflict with, such as when we're face to face with somebody whom we really can't stand. Or who at the very least makes us uncomfortable. Perhaps it's because we have "history"—that code word for unhappy times. Such as I do with my former wife. We were married a long time and have been apart even longer. But seeing her often brings up a lot of unease. Some of it has to do with the reasons for the divorce. Some of it has to do with the fact of our marriage and how we interacted. Every little hurt inflicted or received floods back. It's not a matter of blame; it's a matter of discomfort. But our history together makes it harder for me to be nice to her in the same way that I could to someone I met just a few days earlier with whom I have no history.

That's when I have to step outside of myself, lower my defenses, and remember that at one time we were in love and we stood before a gathering of our friends and family and God and pledged our lives to each other. That it didn't work is a tragedy, for which I bear a big responsibility. God loved us both at that wedding and God loves us both still. And when I remember her as a beloved child of God, and know her family situations with me and since then, then a peacefulness comes to me that enables me to see the Light of God in her. It lets me pray for her. Not that I'm better or more holy—for all I know, she's praying for me.

> I L L U M I N A T I N G   M O M E N T
> Breathe deeply.
> Relax your body and mind.
> Think about the following slowly and gently.
> Savor each thought.
> *As I think about the people in my life at this moment, who among them could use a passionate thought?*

Walking around St. John's University in Collegeville, Minnesota, I came upon a plaque that said, "Let all guests who arrive be received as Christ, because He will say: 'I was a stranger and you took Me in' (Mt 25:35). And let due honor be shown to all, especially to those 'of the household of the faith' (Gal 6:10) and to wayfarers."

"Let all guests who arrive be received as Christ" is one of the most familiar and quoted phrases of the Rule of St. Benedict. It emphasizes the paramount place that hospitality occupies in a Benedictine monastery. It's a hospitality that goes beyond the expected social graces—those smiles and kind greetings that we have for expected guests. And it says something about Minding the Light in others. I often have to ask myself if I receive all my guests the same way as I would receive Christ. I'm pretty sure I don't. My vision of God in others is not quite as clear as that of Dorothy Day, who once wrote:

> Christ is always with us, always asking for room in our hearts. . . . But now it is with the voice of our contemporaries that He speaks, with the eyes of store clerks, factory workers, and children that He gazes; with the hands of office workers, slum dwellers, and suburban housewives that He gives. If we hadn't got Christ's own words for it, it would seem raving lunacy to believe . . . that my guest is Christ. There is nothing to show it, perhaps. There are no halos already glowing round their heads—at least none that human eyes can see. . . . It would be foolish to pretend that it is always easy to remember this. If everyone were holy and handsome, with "alter Christus" shining in neon lighting from them, it would be easy to see Christ in everyone.

Sometimes I forget to look for the holy or the handsome in the way God defines those words. When I do Mind the Light of God in other people, I am reminded of things I say I believe, but too often do not think about. One is that I do believe that God created all people in his image. That means that every person I meet, from the president of the foundation that funds my work to the bag boy at the grocery store who wants to talk about how Muslims know that they're exactly facing Mecca when they pray, are both men inherently good and worthy of my love and respect. Every well-dressed man, bag lady, checkout girl, and snot-faced, whiny kid I see today carries a divine spark, the same as I do. And it's easy to envy the well-dressed man, pity the bag lady, glare at the checkout girl for being so slow, and hope the snot-faced, whiny kid doesn't sneeze on me without beholding that they are each created in God's image. God loves all those other people as much as God loves me. Again, this is easy to believe intellectually; it's a little harder to put into heart feelings. A friend sent me an e-mail with a picture of a t-shirt he thought I'd find funny. "Jesus loves you," it says, followed by, "But I'm His Favorite." I did think it was funny—but it also hit a bit too close to home.

The mystery of the Light of Christ in others (as well as us) is that it changes them so that we behold the face of Jesus in them. We are surrounded by God. We live in the midst of God. We miss the chance of beholding God if we do not take time to look for him in the people around us. Dorothy Bass writes about a wise mother who, while tucking her children into bed each night, asks, "Where did you meet God today?"

And they tell her, one by one: A teacher helped me; there was a homeless person in the park; I saw a tree with lots of flowers.

When I first read that story, I asked myself, *Where did I meet God today?* Is my inner sight as gifted as that mother's children? So how do we spot God in others? There is no set formula. We each will come up with ways on our own. Begin by thinking of the things that help you connect to the divine and centered places in your life. Maybe they are things like peace or beauty or joy. Or maybe icons of the suffering Christ bring you close to God. Whatever they are, look for them in the lives and eyes of those you find stepping alongside you on the sidewalk or delivering your mail or asking you for "A coupla bucks to buy a sandwich, buddy?"

We learn to see God in others by learning to care for each other. Singer/songwriter Carrie Newcomer reminds us that we should "treat each other tenderly" for ". . . the arms of God will gather in / each sparrow that falls [and] . . . makes no separation / just fiercely loves us all."

ILLUMINATING MOMENT

Breathe deeply.

Relax your body and mind.

Think about the following slowly and gently.

Savor each thought.

How would it feel to love others fiercely as God does?

If we look for God in others, we find that God also appears in unexpected people in unexpected places. Hey, that's God appearing over the shoulder of the young mother in front of us at the mall. Wait, that's God peeking out from behind the espresso machine. Is that God peering out from under the car while changing the oil? Gerard Manley Hopkins, the nineteenth-century Jesuit poet, knew that it might be when he wrote:

> As kingfishers catch fire, dragonflies draw flame;
> As tumbled over rim in roundy wells . . .
> Christ—for Christ plays in ten thousand places,
> Lovely in limbs, and lovely in eyes not his
> To the Father through the features of men's faces.

If Christ is at play in ten thousand places in lovely limbs and eyes not his, then I can see God all around me all the time. Minding the Light in others teaches that God is wise like the older ladies I visited on my pastoral calls. God is faithful like those few who gather at the meetinghouse on the snowiest Sunday morning of the year. God is prophetic like my friend Kevin's preaching at North Church, extravagantly loving like Nancy at Christmas, and just—but also compassionate—like my friend Mary Lee, the retired judge. These—and other folks—teach me what God is like. As a British Friend, L. Hugh Doncaster, wrote:

> This central affirmation, that the Light of the Christ-like God shines in every person, implies that our knowledge of God is both subjective and

objective. . . . But it is an equally important part of
our faith and practice to recognise that we are not
affirming the existence and priority of your light
and my light, but of the Light of God, and of the
God who is made known to us supremely in Jesus.
. . . It is further checked by the fact that if God is
known in measure by every person, our knowledge
of him will be largely gained through the experience
of others who reverently and humbly seek him.

My parents, Grandpa and Grandma Bill, Uncle Johnny,
Grandma Fortune, Uncle Burt, Aunt Audrey, a parade of
Sunday school teachers, youth group leaders, pastors, and
many more were Christ at play all about me—many times
without their realizing they were molding me, teaching me
about God. Watching them taught me how to love people
and the land, to be honest, to be true, to be loyal, and to be
a blessing.

Christ was also at play in the doofus who cut me off on
the highway, and in the rude deliveryman. They continue to
be unexpected God-sightings. I expect to see God's Light in
those I love and respect. But the unexpected and annoying
sightings, if my eyes are open, are also a blessing, if I allow
them to be.

The people in my life have been urban and rural, rich and
poor, white and people of color, married and not, young and
not, American and not, nice and not. But if I take time to look
for God's Light within them, I see that they all seem to share
two loves—for God (even if God's name was not mentioned)
and for each other (even if it's unrecognized). I find such

love contagious. We all long to be swept up in the mighty passion of an eternal loving-kindness. The closest thing to that on this earth is our Minding God's Light in each other.

CHAPTER FIVE

Incandescence, Fluorescence, and Flashlights

Artificial Light and the Life of the Spirit

"The impact of artificial light on nineteenth-century life was as profound as the impact of digital technology in the twentieth century." Those words come from an article reviewing the exhibit "Light: The Industrial Age 1750-1900: Art & Science, Technology & Society." This exhibit was put together by Louise Lippincott of the Carnegie Museum of Art in Pittsburgh and Andreas Blüm of the Van Gogh Museum in Amsterdam. The two of them began thinking about the impact of artificial light, and their work resulted in exhibitions in Amsterdam and Pittsburgh in 2000–2001.

As they worked on this project, Lippincott and Blüm found that the development of artificial light and the subsequent new lighting methods changed how people saw. That change in seeing changed how people lived. That's because until mass production of light sources such as coal oil, gaslight, and electric lights developed in the nineteenth century, it seemed as if light had been entirely in God's hands. Yes, candles and firelight existed—but these didn't really control light. They illuminated small bits of the darkness. Now, light could pour forth in even the humblest of homes or the meanest of factories. The easy availability of light "got people thinking of light as a material, manipulatable thing, not a gift from God," Lippincott explains. "This was a completely new concept, and it opened up light as a subject for investigation, and for art."

Today most of us go about our business not in the light of day but in the light of Edison. We rarely think about God's being responsible for so profound a gift as light. This makes it hard to understand our recent ancestors' fears that it might be unnatural or even evil to light up our rooms and factories and go on working long after God's sun had set. Yet that's exactly how many nineteenth-century folks felt. In John Martin's 1841 painting "Pandemonium," the palace of Satan is lit by what appears to be gaslights, seemingly related to the flames of hell erupting at the Devil's feet. Some critics say the scene bears a remarkable resemblance to London's Pall Mall, the first street in London to be lit by gas and a favorite playground of libertines.

On the other hand, as the exhibit shows, if light enables new sorts of bad behavior, it also exposes that bad behavior. One example is the nineteenth-century police lantern with its bull's-eye lens. It's perfect for illuminating criminal activity. This sounds sort of like the searchlight aspect of the Inner Light. Cop as God? God as cop?

The exhibit also showed people's change in thinking about light by showing plates made by Gustave Doré for editions of the Bible in 1865 and 1866. In the French edition of 1865, for the text, "And God said, 'Let there be light,'" Doré portrays God as a magnificent figure raising his arm in a burst of sunlight. In the English edition of 1866, in Protestant, industrial England, Dore's God appears as a cloud. France at the time was still largely unartificially lit—England shone bright by the light of man.

While there's no denying that digital technology has had a profound impact (I'm writing this on a computer, after all), the impact of artificial light in our times is as profound as it was in the nineteenth century. We may be used to artificial light, but its impact on how we live is immeasurable. So, too, is its impact on our spirituality. It's just that often we don't recognize or even think about the impact artificial light has on our spirituality.

Even when we're asleep (and sometimes then if we don't have a Clapper or a timer to turn off the lights), we are surrounded by all sorts of artificial light. We have developed ambient light, task lighting, accent lighting, and many more.

As imperfect as they are, these lights help us work and play well, travel at night, visit with friends until the wee hours, and much more. It might seem that, if God is light, then more light means more God. Thanks to light we can clap on and clap off, we could get up earlier or stay up later to read the Bible or pray. Instead, though, more light often means that we cram more activity into our lives than our ancestors ever imagined. Maybe they had reason for concern. With all that busyness it can be easy to lose a sense of God's presence with us. We overwhelm God's lights with our own.

ILLUMINATING MOMENT
Breathe deeply.
Relax your body and mind.
Think about the following slowly and gently.
Savor each thought.
*What impact does artificial light have on
my spirituality?*

Light pollution is one of humankind's newest forms of pollution. Light pollution creeps out from our cities into the skies above—a nocturnal glow arising from the mass of houselights, streetlights, auto lights and more. It's hard to fly over the United States anymore and not see lights—so electrified and lit have we become. All these lights, which are helpful in some instances (we don't want to drive in the dark), blind us to God's other lights: The moon and stars are much less visible in the inner city than they are sixty miles from town. Some studies suggest that ninety-nine percent of people in the continental USA and Western Europe never see a truly dark, starry sky. Light pollution means the sky never gets much darker than it would during natural twilight. We even fool the birds, which serenade false dawns caused by all sorts of bottled light.

It's interesting that we think of bulbs containing such a mystical phenomenon as light, while we miss the mystical presence of God lighting the people and things around us.

Since most of this artificial light involves our workaday world—whether in an office or at home—it helps if we learn to see the holy that is present in this light. One way we see is by beholding those people and things around us as sacred. Just as in natural light, this calls for an intentional way of seeing. We may find such deep seeing easier when we're outdoors— enjoying sunsets or walks in the park. However, for the majority of us, most of our time is spent indoors. We may not see artificial light as lending itself to revelation as easily as we do God's Light. Which is all the more reason to find ways for seeing the sacred around us—whether it is lit by ambient, task, accent, or God's lighting.

This seeing becomes easier if your workplace lets you carve out some space for pictures and other things that connect you with your faith. An electronic decision maker sits on the corner of my desk. Ask a question ("Should I give Adam a raise?"), press a button, the lights blink, and then one of them pops on to light the answer. It's just something silly, but it was my Dad's. When I see it, I stop and think about what a good man he is and strive to be more like him. There's also the "George the Fox" piece by Sally Wern Comport I mentioned earlier, and a drypoint etching, "Study of a Winged Figure," by an artist friend of mine named John Rush. All of these things—silly, whimsical, and serious—help me connect to the sacred. And they are all seen by artificial light. These are all important to me. You probably have things surrounding you that help you connect your workspace with your interior life. If so, celebrate them. If not, you might want to look for ways to bring them into the space your life fills during the workday.

Think about pictures or knickknacks or small books that you could introduce into your workspace: items that would help you Mind the Light. Much of Nancy's indoor work takes place in the kitchen. Since Nancy is blessed with a gift for hospitality, one of her spiritual reminders hangs over the kitchen sink. It is a tile inscribed with "The Kitchen Prayer."

> Lord of all pots and pans, and things, since I've no time to be
> A saint by doing lovely things or watching late with Thee . . .
> Make me a saint by getting meals and washing up the plates.
> Although I must have Martha's hands, I have a Mary mind . . .
> Accept the service that I do. I do it unto Thee.

Even if you're not permitted to have overtly religious pictures or symbols, there may be a way to have a piece or two that helps you connect in an indirect way with the divine. That's what my decision maker does for me. It connects me with my dad and through him to God.

Seeing in artificial light is also easier when we see those around us as people filled with extraordinary giftedness. This isn't always easy—especially when that extraordinarily gifted person is also extraordinarily annoying. But by beholding their giftedness, we then find it easier to see them as called to the same work we are. They embody some of the same spiritual values we do—integrity, honesty, love, kindness, and respect—that's why many of them are there. Work, for many of us, is more than a paycheck. This is true whether our work is overtly spiritual or not. It may be easy to think this way about a large pastoral staff gathering for prayer at a candlelit altar. But, as spiritual people making our way in the world, we are also called in some mysterious way to miraculous work—even if it's lit by four-bulb fluorescent overhead fixtures or sparks flying off a machine grinder. When we learn to see our work and the others working with us, then we become grateful for them—and we may even learn to say thank you for the work they do and the skills and passions they bring to our joint work. Such an attitude, even under the glare of a drafting-table light, helps our spiritual development. By the task lighting around us, we see God present in our work.

ILLUMINATING MOMENT
Breathe deeply.
Relax your body and mind.
Think about the following slowly and gently.
Savor each thought.
What are some ways I can Mind the Light at work?

"We may as well go home," I said, easing the car into the dark parking lot. "Electricity's out." It was Christmas Eve, and we had just driven more than two hundred miles from my parents' house to get back in time for our Meeting's candlelight service. As we came down the main drag of Plainfield, I noticed that the west end of town was dark, except for some police-car lights flashing in the town's three intersections. Light. Then no light. The meetinghouse windows, normally aglow from the lights within, were black.

"It's a candlelight service," Nancy chided. "Tonight we'll just have to do the whole thing by candlelight instead of lighting them at the end." So the pastor, Nancy, and I scavenged for big candles to light our darkness. Nancy remembered a unity candle left over from a wedding. I knew there were some candles atop the library bookshelves. Bill, the pastor, found some in various drawers around the meetinghouse. By the time we had our few lights lit, there was enough light on the pulpit for him to read his Bible and other passages, for the pianist to see the music for the carols, and for the rest of us to find our way into the pews without banging our shins.

People lit their candles in the foyer and made their way to the meetingroom. I stayed behind with my candle to help any latecomers. When I heard the first carol end and a Scripture passage being read, I stepped outside. The windows were aglow again—softer than usual, but still shining a light in the darkness. I smiled and made my way back in. As I settled in next to Nancy, with the soft, golden glow of candlelight filling the room, the words of a magical night long ago came to life in the readings and in the sound of the baby in front of me snuffling in his sleep. "The little lord Jesus, asleep in the hay," we sang. As the service ended, Nancy nudged me and said, "And you wanted to go home. Think of what we would have missed."

I don't usually think of candlelight as artificial light—to me, artificial light is usually a sealed bulb of tungsten filament, neon, fluorescence, laser, or mercury. But that night I realized

that candlelight's soft, flickering flame was one of the first
artificial lights. And such soft, flickering flames have lit countless
worship services through the ages—vespers, compline,
matins. The advent of gaslight and electric light enabled
evening services in many churches. Today, or more
appropriately, tonight, we can use the artificial lights
available to us for our spiritual development. My workday
is pretty crowded. I try to start each day with a reading or
prayer before I settle in for the business of the day. But
after that, besides grabbling a minute or two for prayer,
my spiritual reading has to happen in the evenings. That's
when I have time to take a piece of writing and really sit
with it. And I do so by a 75-watt GE bulb burning away in
a table lamp next to my chair.

The artificial light of my computer screen sometimes calls
me to prayer. Our congregation has an e-mail prayer chain.
So we get notices throughout the day and night that, thanks
to the brightly glowing pixels on my screen, alert me to a
joy or a sorrow. They invite me to take some time away
from the important work I'm doing to do some really
important work. So, with a dip of my head and a brief closing
of my eyes, I offer an LCD-lit litany of petition or praise.

Computer-generated e-mail prayer requests, spiritual
reading by electric light, prayer services by candlelight:
These are some of the ways artificial light helps me feed my
soul. As you think about living soulfully by artificial light,
you will probably come up with a very different list. Those
differences don't matter. What does matter is discovering
ways to use the light you've been given—including artificial
light—to light your way.

> ILLUMINATING MOMENT
> Breathe deeply.
> Relax your body and mind.
> Think about the following slowly and gently.
> Savor each thought.
> *How can I use human-made light to feed my soul?*

Artificial lights filled that night. The first was the message light blinking on our answering machine. After finding someone to help her at night with her failing father, Nancy's brother Jimmy agreed to come from 4 to 10 PM. For the first time in years, Nancy could spend evenings at home and have supper with me and relax before the next day's care. "Jimmy has to leave early," she said in a low voice, looking at the blinking light. After three years of her spending most of her time at her dad's farm without help, I didn't care for the reason. We had supper in stony silence. At 7 o'clock, with the sun setting and lamps turning on, she left. I turned on the television. "7:03," said the little time stamp at the bottom of the set. I turned on the lamp behind me and turned off the television. I listened to Chris Isaak and Neil Young, watching the LCD counter display the tracks on the CDs. Electronic number mounted on electronic number. The VCR announced time passing—7:35, 8:10, 8:40. About the time the VCR announced 9:15, I turned the lamp down. The room softened. I read awhile longer. I looked up, softer inside than I had been. 9:45. Nancy would be home at 10 or shortly after that, depending on when the night person arrived.

I stood and looked out of our dining room windows. I could see her dad's house across the pasture. I picked out a living-room light. I decided to make the hike down our gravel driveway and walk her home. It was late, and the forecasted low was in the high thirties. I pulled out our rechargeable flashlight and begin walking toward the back porch. 9:50, the microwave's LCD clock broadcast. The screen door smacked shut behind me as I flipped the flashlight switch and cast a feeble beam down the driveway.

As I neared the road between our home and Nancy's dad's house, I flicked the flashlight beam through the budding bushes in front of the farmhouse. The weak light illuminated Nancy's old convertible. She'd driven over. *I may as well head back*, I thought, turning off the flashlight. The mercury light in the barn lot lit the rest of the yard with quasi-daylight. I looked up at the house and saw that there were more lights on than usual. Including her dad's bedroom light. *I may as well go in and then let her drive me home, when the night nurse comes. Mend some barbed-wire fences.* As I walked into the semi-lit yard, I looked into his bedroom. The ceiling light blazed, and it showed Nancy pacing back and forth. *I hope he's not yelling at her—not at this hour.*

I opened the sticking back door, making the old bell attached to it tinkle. Before I could say I was sorry, Nancy came through the kitchen and launched herself into my arms, sobbing. "Daddy's dead, Daddy's dead. I tried to call. Where were you?"

Soon every light downstairs was lit while we made the dreaded late-night bad news calls to family members.

Headlights racing down the county road and slowing to turn into the farm lot announced sons and grandchildren's arrivals. The farmhouse shone bright in the night—as if to ward off the angel of death, though he had not passed over.

Almost every event that evening had or been marked by human-made light—from LCDs computing the time and CD tracks to old lamps burning multiple sixty-watt bulbs. That's not unusual. Most of our lives are spent under artificial light. Sometimes those lights tell us that we have messages or light the way down a dark country driveway. Sometimes the light lights the tragic—the smoke alarm blinking or a flat line on a heart monitor hooked up to someone we love. Sometimes artificial light illuminates both good and tragic—one family at one end of the brightly lit emergency room getting the happy news that their sixteen-year-old son will survive the accident while at the other end other parents hearing their daughter has just died. Sometimes we pay attention to all the lights. I did that night. They marked everything from CD tracks to a message I didn't want to time passing by. But if we just see them, and there's no love in that seeing, then it's easy to miss any meaning that might be there. The thing that saved me that night was looking out and seeing the farmhouse lights. I loved the people in that farmhouse—even Nancy's rascally old dad, who was often hard for me to love. The lights called me to walk across the road. And so the screen door slammed behind me at the same time Nancy was leaving a mournful message on the machine, pleading, "Where are you? I need you."

> ILLUMINATING MOMENT
> Breathe deeply.
> Relax your body and mind.
> Think about the following slowly and gently.
> Savor each thought.
> *What time can I remember when artificial light marked an emotional or a spiritual experience?*

In addition to the artificial lights that light our work, there all kinds of lights for health—including some that affect our spiritual life as well. It's believed that Seasonal Affective Disorder (SAD) is caused by the lack of bright light. I know I get blue when there are too many cloudy days in a row, and SAD makes my blues look like a walk in a sunny park. The best way found for treating it, short of going to a brightly lit climate, which many of us can't do easily, is to use a light box or a similar therapy device. The optimal light level for this therapy is light that is about as bright as a spring morning on a clear day. And it only takes fifteen to thirty minutes a day to alleviate the SAD symptoms. Just as with God's spring morning light, you don't have to stare at the light (you can read or listen to music) to get the full effect. You just have to allow the light to reach your eyes.

Light therapy is now also used for treating many types of cancer. Researchers at University College London Hospital in England used it on fourteen men whose prostate cancer had come back after being treated with radiation. First the patients got an intravenous injection of a photosensitive drug, and then researchers waited three days for the drug to migrate to the tumor. Next, doctors shone light on the tumor, activating the photosensitive drug, which then destroyed the tumor. With further refinements, researchers think that light therapy can be used to destroy prostate cancer with few complications.

In these two cases, humans have used our ability to manufacture light to help our fellows. It's a different kind of sharing God's Light perhaps, but a unique one in that this use of light for healing people has allowed them to become co-creators with God, to replicate God's caring in uniquely, humanly inventive ways.

We also know that even informal, nonmedical light therapy lifts our spirits and turns us toward the Light. I am not partial to holiday displays. My idea of a tasteful display is a sidewalk lit with luminaries. But as I drive around during Christmas time I see displays that make Clark Griswold of "National Lampoon's Christmas Vacation" fame look like a slacker. I think such things are way over the top. Then I read a sermon preached by the Reverend C. Irving Cummings of Old Cambridge Baptist Church that made me think about it a bit differently. In his sermon he says this:

> For this year, for the first time, it occurred to me that this annual explosion of light on people's front lawns and housetops is more than pretty or garish holiday decoration. This year, for the first time, I began to see it as an expression of what the

anthropologists call "sympathetic magic." . . . How did it never occur to me before that our putting out Christmas lights hails from a . . . thing that goes back thousands of years, in nearly every culture imaginable? The enshrouding dark of this season is a frightening thing, especially this year. There's a little piece of the brain that wonders, really, "Will the light return?" This year, there is, for me at least, a visceral connection with those thousands upon thousands of human ancestors who burned hilltop night fires in order to lure back the sun. . . . Or, who brought Yule Logs into their homes. Or, who lit candles on trees in the midst of nowhere.

This year, thanks to C. Irving, I'm looking at the lights differently, too. They help me see my neighbors in a different way. For one thing, the holiday lights help me see my neighbors. Most of the year, tucked back into the corner of our field and nestled tight against the woods as we are, we can't see any houses, except Nancy's family's farm place across the field from us. But now, with the leaves stripped from the trees, I can see Gene Mitchell's brightly colored house half a mile away. A white-lighted house a mile behind ours shines atop a hill and reflects in a lake between them and us. I feel a kinship to them both—even the mile-away neighbors who I'll likely never meet, as our country roads truly never cross. Seeing the lights gleaming in the dark, cold, winter nights, connects me with my human family. And through them to God. A connection never possible sans artificial—even if garish—light.

> I L L U M I N A T I N G   M O M E N T
> Breathe deeply.
> Relax your body and mind.
> Think about the following slowly and gently.
> Savor each thought.
> *When has artificial light been healing to me?*

I admit that I prefer God's natural light to human light. It feels better on my soul and skin. I am enough of a curmudgeon that I tend to agree with a letter written in 1919 to the editor of the *Scientific American* by C. W. Browne of Kansas City. In it Mr. Browne writes, "If you will try it out personally, observing the hours that govern the city clerk or laboring man, I believe that you will decide that God knows more about time than President Wilson does." Even though that letter's almost a century old, I think God does know more about time and light than do we. And for the sakes of our souls, while we rejoice and work and play in the light that's been given us by GE, Sylvania, Phillips, and Kmart blue-light specials, we feed our souls if we find ways to turn toward God's Light at least a bit each day.

Life and the lights in it are rarely either/or propositions. We do not generally spend life wholly in either artificial or natural light. Usually it is some combination of the two. I was reminded of that while attending the annual ministry of writing conference at Earlham School of Religion. Every writing conference there begins with worship. The seminary's meetingroom has lots of windows. It's a two-story space.

Windows line three of the four walls of both the first and second stories. As I walked into the meetingroom, I settled into a bench (no pews for us Friendly folk) that faced the southern bank of windows. The windowless north wall was behind me. I knew that for the next hour I could watch the autumn sun track its lazy way through the mix of clouds and clear. The light at the end of the sixty minutes would be different from the light at the start.

Sitting in the middle of the room was a small table with a flickering candle atop it—pointing us to the Light of Christ, which, when we are silent and still in body and soul, illuminates us all.

I settled into the silence in my usual manner as the room quietly filled. I took off my glasses, scooted around on the bench to get comfortable, and crossed my legs—my best posture for worship. I felt the silence wash over me and through my closed eyes sensed the sun moving in and out of cloud cover. After about thirty minutes I felt led to open my eyes and put my glasses back on.

The sun played hide-and-seek with the alternately cloudy and clear sky. Soft light suffused the room, and then suddenly the people sitting there were etched in stark shadows and brilliant light: a living bas-relief. I turned my eyes upward, to watch the clouds float across one southern window, pass behind the wall, and then into the other window frame, and slowly swallow the sun. I looked down to the first-story windows lining the room. Out the one directly across from me blazed a maple in glorious reds and oranges—afire in the mid-morning fall light.

Then the light through the upper windows went soft as clouds filled the sky. I saw the people slide from relief into focus. Facing me across the room sat a woman I knew who had moved from New England and left her law practice to attend seminary. I glanced to my right. There sat a writing friend who had heard earlier that week that the editing position she'd held for eight years had been eliminated in a cost-savings move. My friend in front of me, gray hair steely in the soft light, had just become a grandfather for the first time a few days earlier. All around me I saw God's beloved human creation lit by God's Light.

Through it all, the candle cast its light. *Competing—or complementing—the sun?* I wondered. Sometimes, as the sky cleared, the candlelight seemed to dim. At others, when the cloud filled the sky, the candle seemed bright.

I thought about how much of my life was like that—a mix of lights. Each, in its way, was illuminating what was not seen by the light of the other. Each was a blessing. Each was a call to pay attention—to God's Light wherever and however it comes.

This brings me to an old joke. "How many Quakers does it take to change a lightbulb?" The answer this time is, "None. Who needs a lightbulb when you have the Inner Light?" That is true for all of us—not just Friends.

※

CHAPTER SIX

Light for the Journey
Seeing Our Path to God

The night air whipped around us as we roared down the country road. Nancy and I were returning from a day of driving our MG on an over-the-road rally across south-central Indiana. The old British sports car was a gift from my dad a few years earlier. I'd been riding in or driving that old car since I was a little kid. I never got tired of it—the growl of the exhaust, the smell of hot oil, bugs splattered across the flat windshield. The old headlights pierced the gathering ground fog, lighting the road ahead of us. Then suddenly they didn't. Everything went black. Country road black. No streetlights out here. I slowed, and we crept toward the lone stoplight gleaming in the distance. The road had a wide shoulder there, so I pulled over.

I'm no mechanic or electrical engineer. But owning an antique automobile means you learn some things about keeping it running and lit. I opened up the bonnet (we call it a hood here in the U.S.). I peered inside, the only light coming from the now red traffic light. *Why hadn't I stuck a flashlight in the car?* I wiggled the wires coming from the battery. Nothing. There are only two fuses (no power windows, heater, radio, or anything like that in this car), and they both looked okay. I pushed my cap back, screwed up my face, and tried to think. We were five miles from home, and I didn't want to try to drive them without lights. I reached into the under-bonnet toolbox, took out the hammer that I use to knock off the wire wheels for tire changes, and whacked a battery terminal. The lights came back on. And stayed on. Happy with my electrical prowess, I put the hammer back, closed up the car, hopped in and drove uneventfully, but lit, home.

Life is like that sometimes. We zip along. Everything's fine and light. Then suddenly it's not. A child gets sick. A job is lost. Someone dies. We're plunged into blackness. And then the question becomes, how to find light in this darkness?

ILLUMINATING MOMENT
Breathe deeply.
Relax your body and mind.
Think about the following slowly and gently.
Savor each thought.
When was a time when the lights went out for me?
What did I do to find light?

It was a sunny summer Sunday morning, and that made the ugliness of what happened that day all the more jarring. Later that morning I wished I'd never opened that door. The smell that seeped out from underneath it should've been a warning. I'd never smelled anything like it before. It smelled so sweet. And so awful.

I opened the bedroom door to tell Greg, my best friend, goodbye. But it looked like he was still asleep. It also looked like he'd been drinking again. Red wine was splashed all over one side of his face and clothes. "Spilt wine and summer humidity," I thought. "That's what that smell is."

I decided to look for the bottle, wake him, and tell him to clean himself up. As I walked closer, I noticed the wine seemed awfully thick. And it had other stuff in it. It wasn't wine that was spilled all over Greg. It was Greg spilled all over Greg. As he lay on his bed, the spillage came from the right side of his head being blown off. He'd shot himself Saturday afternoon with a .38 revolver. What I had thought was cheap red wine was really a sticky-looking red, gray, gooey mess of blood, brain tissue, and other body fluids. That's what caused the awful and sweet smell.

What happened next is still a blur of frantic phone calls, police officers, and paramedics standing around talking in low, bored tones. What was left of Greg was carried carelessly down the stairs inside a body bag leaking dark red blood all over the deep green carpet. That bright July day was the darkest day of my twenty-four years of life.

The darkness did not ease for a while. This is no tale of finding a light switch, flipping it, light flooding my soul, and everything suddenly being perfect. It didn't happen that way. But points of light did come to me that helped through that time.

One point of light was learning to take care of myself. I was a wreck. It was hard to eat, sleep, and go to work.

Some things I had to do. I had to go to work. We needed the money. Other things I didn't have to do. I didn't have to stay up and watch late-night television—I needed to get some sleep. Music helped me sleep. So I'd put headphones on and fall asleep listening to music. I read things I wanted to read. People gave me articles and books to read—but most of them were heavy on grief therapy or theology. Instead I read silliness, including a *faux* cookbook entitled *Moose Mousse and Other Exotic Recipes* by Robert Gilbert. A retreat into nonsense helped more in the short run than did wading out into the depths of intellectual exploration of grieving. I took control of my own care, doing what needed to be done to strengthen my physical, emotional, and spiritual self.

This didn't happen easily. I wasn't a quick learner about emotional life. But Greg's suicide forced me to learn to use the wisdom that I had gained in my short lifetime to figure out the best ways to care for myself in that dark time. That time taught me that we know as well or better than others the things that help us feel connected to God's Light. As we do them, we discover that hope is there. Not in an easy, greeting-card sort of way, but in a way that matters—that gives us strength deep within and far outside. Light comes in the care we give ourselves. The books, music, naps, and even playing softball helped me see that while one important light in my life had been tragically snuffed out, God's Light still shone around and within me.

Other points of light came from friends. Greg's suicide happened the day after I'd been giving a sermon and a presentation on youth ministry. I was a minister. And yet, I found myself in a position to be ministered to. This was hard for me. I was the strong one, the one to whom people turned. But I had nothing to give. I was spent, wrung out. I needed care.

Friends brought light in that situation. Not so much through what they said, but through simply being there. The unexpected visits, invitations out for ice cream, a thinking-of-you letter appearing in the mail. Each of those things helped lighten a gloom that felt enveloping and dense. One way of finding light in the midst of darkness is learning to sense God's presence coming in the form of others helping you. Letting them care. Letting them tend you. Letting their prayers be your prayers. Letting their sense of God's presence be your sense. Letting your friends hold you up when you feel that you might be sinking. In our friends' buoyancy, we might begin to see small glimmers of God's Light through theirs.

Another point of light for me was my spiritual friends. These were not always the same people as my "regular" friends, though often there was overlap. I talked to folk I knew had deep faith even though they'd gone through deep trials. These wise friends didn't rush me or tell me how to feel. Instead, they listened and cared and prayed and cried. They reassured me of their great love for me, thereby reminding me of God's love. They were spiritually astute enough to be open and vulnerable about their own faith and pain. In so doing they brought the Light of Christ to me. And I came to trust them. Perhaps that's because, as Emily Dickinson said, "When Jesus tells us about his Father, we distrust him. When he shows us his Home, we turn away, but when he confides to us that he is 'acquainted with Grief,' we listen, for that also is an Acquaintance of our own." I listened to these friends as emissaries of the Light because they were acquainted with grief, which was an acquaintance of my own.

They spoke words when words were needed, but also kept silence when silence was called for. Later, at other desperate times of my life, I began to see that becoming a spiritual friend was a sign of spiritual maturity—of learning to grow in the Light. John Punshon, an English Friend and a friend of mine said:

> I came to realize that the best way to deepen my love of God was to use my experience of the love in my everyday life in all its variety, subtlety, and uncertainty. Getting on with those I love is often a business demanding patience, discretion, tact, and understanding. It gets complicated sometimes. It also gets strained, occasionally to the breaking point. But without expression it is barren. I show my love in the things I do, and I also show it by words of endearment.

"Getting on with those we love" is a demanding business, especially in the dark days of life. But those who are wise use their experiences of everyday life, with all its variety of joys and sorrows, to help us along our pilgrim way. The light of wise women and men helped guide me through some of my dark days.

Yet another point of light was my belief in God. I found that my faith was more robust than I had imagined. Not that it wasn't buffeted, but rather the buffeting didn't destroy my faith or me. I found I didn't have time for platitudes or the countless other semi-religious stupid things that people say in the midst of tragedy—"Oh, God must have needed another angel" or "It was God's will." That was drivel—so much nonsense. Greg's death was a tragedy, that's all, and that's too much. God didn't will Greg to be in so much pain that he saw suicide as the only way of relieving that pain. Such talk was especially hard to take from supposedly spiritual people. It was then I found that my faith was moving beyond a place of easy answers into a harder place where I could live in the questions. And, instead of being less secure, my questioning faith became a safer place. That's because it acknowledged the reality of my life and Greg's death. I began to find comfort in readings by people of faith who knew that wrestling with the whys of life and with God put them in good company. Job of old, for instance. And Zoe White of today. She has experienced tragedy, so I trusted Zoe's words when I read:

> On the morning of Frances' death, as I stood by her bedside, I made a secret resolve somewhere deep in my being which has only recently come to the surface. I made an agreement with God that from that day onward, everything I have to say about God, everything I have to say theologically, has to stand with me by Frances' bedside. If it cannot stand at the side of death, if it cannot stand by the side of a fifty-five-year-old woman who wanted to live to see the trees again, it had better not stand at all because it is probably not worth very much.

Likewise, if everything I have to say about God cannot stand by the side of a twenty-four-year-old man who *never* wanted to see the trees again, it better not stand at all because it is probably not worth very much then, either. Words like Zoe's brought me light—and taught me to be sensitive, too, in pastoral situations where tragedy often visited and left wrecked lives. I learned to pray in a new way, asking God merely to walk with me without pleading for God to take all the pain away. In that I discovered what the Psalmist knew long ago—that light and dark made no difference to God's presence with us. "Where can I go from your Spirit?. . . If I say, 'Surely the darkness will hide me and the light become night around me,' even the darkness will not be dark to you; the night will shine like the day, for darkness is as light to you." So when we need to, we should go ahead and grieve and cry and scream and kick whenever we're in the valley of the shadow. None of those things have anything to do with denying the realities of faith. Rather they have to do with being fully human and fully alive. Part of being human, for better or worse, means having hurting hearts. As one Quaker once wrote:

> A God we cannot be honest with is no God. If we bow the head and say, Thy will be done, when our heart is aflame with protest, we only increase our own pain. Better to rail, rail on God at the passing into the night of this small sweet innocence than to assume unreal acceptance. And then, with small steps, treading the way of sorrows, we may gradually, or perhaps with blinding suddenness, look up from the

dark road and see—see that He has been treading the Way with us, holding us when we faltered, giving us the strength to go hesitatingly forward.

A final point of light for me was memory. Bits of light broke through when I remembered riding in Greg's hulking Oldsmobile convertible with the top down, sun shining on us, laughing, and being silly. And meeting him in the fifth grade and spending summer afternoons playing "Risk" while lying on the cool concrete of his shaded front porch. Of our graduation from high school. Yes, I mourned him. I still do. I find myself after all these years wondering what kind of life this gifted, kind, smart, funny guy would have had, and mourning the tragedy afresh. And I thank God for the light Greg brought, and brings, into my life.

I L L U M I N A T I N G   M O M E N T
Breathe deeply.
Relax your body and mind.
Think about the following slowly and gently.
Savor each thought.
How have I found light in the darkness?

A neighbor gave me a battered old camera to take on my first trip abroad to Switzerland, and a friend who had access to the darkroom at school helped me develop my films when I returned. It made a deep impression on me in the faint reddish glow to

see the image of the village church at Seewis appear
mysteriously from nowhere in the chemical bath,
and then to hang the photograph up to dry. Prayer
for me is like that. The door has to stay shut for the
process to "work." We bring to prayer our memories
and images from scripture and worship that are
usually as difficult to decipher as photographic
negatives. But in the special conditions of the darkroom we can develop them, and the true images can
emerge from the negatives.

Martin L. Smith, an Episcopal priest on the staff of the
United States Holocaust Memorial Museum, wrote those
words. His thoughts on "The Secret Darkroom of the
Heart," as he titled his article, helped me think about the
spiritual nature of dark.

It wasn't until I got to college and worked as a photographer
on the school newspaper and began taking photography
courses that I learned why darkrooms were dark and what
the different lights did in there. I knew that film was light
sensitive, and everybody I knew hunched over their cameras,
whether Nikons or Kodak Brownies, while loading
Kodacolor film. But understanding when light and what
kind of light was safe was something new. I soon learned
that real darkrooms had to be light-tight. If I could stand in
the dark for fifteen minutes, hold a sheet of white paper up
in front of me and see it, then the dark wasn't dark enough.
Once I made it dark enough, then the only light I could use
was a safelight. Safelights cast barely enough of a certain
kind of light to see by. Safelights, often casting a reddish-

orange hue, are designed not to ruin photo paper. True photographic paper—not the kind that we run through our inkjets for digital pictures today—is extremely light sensitive.

The only other light in the darkroom was the enlarger—a large contraption with a light bulb, a negative holder, a lens, and some way of adjusting them to project an image through a negative onto a piece of photographic paper. There are times that neither the enlarger nor the safelight can be on, though. One of those times for me was when, being the frugal Friend that I am, I rolled my own film. I had friends who rolled other things back then, but my vice was buying film in bulk and using reusable film canisters to save money. To do that meant I had to go into a completely dark darkroom. No safelights. The other time was when unloading the film from the canister to put in the developing tank. Pop the top of the film canister, pull out the spool, unwind the spool, wind the film onto the developing tank spool (making sure none of the film touched other parts of the film—if it did, the chemicals couldn't wash over and develop it), and pop the light-proof top onto the tank.

All of this dark just so the work I had done with light could be revealed. As I said, sometimes I had a safelight in the darkroom. A little bit of light to light the way. At others it was completely dark. The preacher in me wants to shout, "Look, a metaphor for life—sometimes lots of light, at other times a tiny glow, and at others blackness all around us." I began to see that in my life, as in the darkroom, work was going on. Something creative was happening. Sometimes, as in the darkroom, it was a negative, like my troubled marriage. At other times it was a powerful, positive swimming up out of the soup, like the care-filled college professor who guided my spiritual and intellectual development. Sometimes it seemed like wasted photo paper and film, like my job in between ministry positions selling photocopiers. And yet, I found that no moment in my life was wasted—in the light or dark. The negatives and positives all shaped me into the person I am today. All the things that happened in the secret darkroom of the heart have helped illuminate the rest of my life.

Before that begins to sound like a really bad country song ("Life Left Me in the Dark, Then I Saw the Light"), I am not saying that I welcomed all the dark times. I still don't. I prefer joy to pain—even a pain that I can learn something from. In that, I'm a lot like the English Friend T. Edmund Harvey, who wrote:

> I am far from having arrived at the mount of vision where so many more faithful disciples have stood, above all mists of doubt. . . yet to think of Christ has meant again and again a parting in the clouds through which a beam of light comes gleaming. Sometimes that light has shone into my vision reflected from word or deed of some man or woman who themselves have been illumined by the same Lord; sometimes the echo of his words in the New Testament; the impress of what he did, above all of what he was, and is and will be, has brought the help I needed.

Another person who learned that good, if hard, work goes on in the dark, is Kathleen Lonsdale. Lonsdale had the light of being one of the first two women to be elected a Fellow of the Royal Society. She was also the first woman President of the British Association for the Advancement of Science. Her darkness came when she volunteered to do fire-watching in London during the blitz of World War II. This bit of selflessness took her to prison. A Quaker, Lonsdale refused to register for civil defense duties. She wanted to help, but would not take the oaths and fill out the forms—not because she was contrary, but because, as a part of our understanding of Jesus' teachings, Friends don't take oaths. So the British authorities sent her to jail. Out of her joys and sorrows, she wrote that:

> It is difficult for us to reconcile the two ideas of God as a loving Father and as the creator of all things, because of the existence of cruelty and undeserved suffering in Nature itself. . . . But that doesn't worry me now, because I have learned, as a scientist, how much I don't understand. I have learned too that when a scientist encounters two apparently irreconcilable ideas, these are stepping stones to new knowledge, and I have confidence there is an answer, even though I may never know it.

There is much I want to understand that I never will. Dark and light, two apparently irreconcilable ideas, have been stepping-stones into knowledge for me. And both have taught me things that I wouldn't have learned if I lived solely in the brilliance of day.

```
ILLUMINATING MOMENT
Breathe deeply.
Relax your body and mind.
Think about the following slowly and gently.
Savor each thought.
What is one lesson I learned in the dark?
```

Another way of finding light in darkness is to think of darkness as what artists call negative space. Negative space is the space between objects, or its parts, or around it. In a painting or drawing, the space around the object is just as important as the piece itself. A good artist strives for balance between the positive (the object) space and the negative (background) space around it. Does a negative space have shape? Sure it does. Hold your hand up in front of your face and spread your fingers. You see the skin, wrinkled knuckles, tiny hairs, and nails needing a trim. Do you see anything else—such as space between your fingers? The positive spaces are those filled by the back of your hand, the fingers, and your thumb—the main subjects of your "work." The negative spaces are the areas around and behind the positive spaces. In my case, while doing this, I see the gold wall of my study between my fingers. If I took a picture of my hand or did a painting of it, I couldn't represent the hand without the negative space. The positive, in art, can't exist without the negative. As Lucia A. Salemme says, "There's an ambiguity in the terms positive and negative space, since the two go together. You cannot possibly see positive space unless there is also a negative space, for the two are permanently linked to one another."

One of my favorite Indiana artists is C. R. Schiefer, a self-taught artist who does wonderful work with limestone. He makes especially good use of negative spaces—carving away limestone to tell a visual story. A good example of negative space is his sculpture "Pushing for Life." "Pushing for Life" is a mostly solid smooth limestone sculpture about five-feet high by two-feet wide and four-to five-inches deep atop stacked, curving bases. Sensuously carved, it's an impression of a woman's torso, soft breasts sloping, stomach swelling, and buttocks tight. Carved out of the lower part of the limestone, is an upside-down fetus. Its head points toward the pelvis and its feet stretch toward the heart. The sculpture calls out to be touched (Schiefer names his work "The Touchables") while telling the story primarily through what's not there rather than what is present. He turns the concept of negative space into a positive one—one that teaches by telling a story. But only if the negative space is paid attention to.

Negative space in the life of the spirit can appear in a number of forms. Some people experience negative space as the *via negativa*. This is a way of describing God through negation. In the via negativa, no words may be used to explain God—God is not this or that. That's because the via negativa holds that any attempt to represent God is flawed and risks limiting the Almighty. The via negativa works at stripping our minds of false descriptions of God and letting our souls define God by our experience.

For other people, the negative space of the spirit comes through the "dark night of the soul." The "dark night of the soul" was understood by the sixteenth-century Spanish poet and Roman Catholic mystic Saint John of the Cross, who first named it as a stage on the mystic path to God. The dark night occurs when those who long to be close to God suffer trials, are afraid that all their spiritual blessings are over, and feel that God has abandoned them. Emptiness and abandonment in this dark night are risks Saint John of the Cross believed have to be undertaken to ready the soul for real union with God. In this context, God's intentional non-presence or withholding presence ultimately leads a person through the darkness into the divine Light. The negative space in the dark night of the soul is a holding place, where inner spiritual work occurs. Seen as negative spaces of the soul, both the via negativa and the dark night of the soul remind us that darkness is not dark to God in the same way it is for us.

The via negativa, learning to describe God through experience rather than words, is similar to learning to see by black light rather than natural light. Black light is the popular name for ultra-violet light. Ultra-violet means "beyond violet." Violet is the color of the shortest wave-lengths of humanly visible light. UV, or black light, is invisible to humans. Some animals and insects can see further into that range than can we. Black light has lots of useful purposes— sterilizing medical equipment, testing antiques for authenticity, and making semiconductors—but most of us are familiar with it through seeing posters and paintings come eerily to life when the natural light is shut off and the black light turned on. This was way cool when I was in high school and college. It was so way cool that one of my friends convinced his parents to let him paint his bedroom black and light it only with black lights. His folks were much more open-minded than mine.

The idea that the use of modern paint on a "classic" oil by Rembrandt or that the weird details of UV Elvis are revealed only by black light helps me see how the via negativa is the black light of the soul. I am used to describing God—who is ultimately indescribable—in words. Loving. Just. Powerful. All-knowing. I have a more difficult time describing God through experience. Yet, just as black light excites the atoms in UV Elvis and brings him into view, so too does the via negativa excite my soul as I try to express my feelings and thoughts about God through the lens of spiritual experience.

The dark night of the soul, though, is not like stepping into a room, closing the blinds, and flipping on a black light. It is more like stepping into a room and having someone else close the blinds. And curtains. And shutters inside and out. And all switches have been removed. But in the same way even in the "real" room, light can be sensed, if not fully seen, so too can it be present in the soul's room.

When I enter a room that is dark, the first thing I do is try to see. I strain and squint in an endeavor to find the light that will lead me safely around the room. Nothing happens. It is when I stand or sit still and quit trying to see that I finally detect a bit of light in the edges. If I turn my head to focus on the light directly, I lose it. I have to look from a different part of my eyes than I usually use. That is true for our soul's sight as well. We may have to content ourselves with the flicker here and glimmer there of God's Light. The Light is indirect. It is almost imperceptible. But it is there— God on the edges.

The dark night of the soul, the via negativa, and other similar experiences are powerful. They teach us the treasures of the dark—lights we've never known before. Lights outside our normal range of vision. They aren't exactly what I'm talking about when I say negative space, though. Negative space, in the artful sense, does mean an absence—an absence of color, an absence of limestone, or an absence of paint. These are absences of material—not essence. Indeed, the essences of negative spaces are used to tell a story more eloquently than something that is present or obvious. Minding the Light guides us in focusing our attention and thereby seeing God in the negative spaces of our lives in a way that color, noise, or material may never reveal. God is present in the negative spaces that make up the paintings and sculptures that are our lives.

Understood that way, negative space is not absence, but a different view of God's presence. Deep seeing informs that negative space. First, Minding the Light leads us into observation. When we get really still, that is. Time seems to slow down, and we can more carefully observe what is present (even in the "holes") around us. Remember those "magic eye" comics that were all the rage in the 1980s (they sold more than 25 million copies worldwide)? You'd hold the stereogram image close to your nose, let your eyes unfocus, move the paper away, and a hidden image swam into view? I never could quite get them! I did them too fast. And that's a point, I think, of finding God in negative spaces of silence. Take your time. Slow down. Look deeply.. In doing so, you'll observe a presence that you had not noticed was there. It's easy to see God in a sunset (yes, it's a cliché, but no less true) and other awe-inspiring sights. It's often harder in an empty room. Or a dark one.

Thomas Kelly, one of the pioneers of modern spirituality, teaches us well about negative space and light and darkness:

> The light for which the world longs is already shining. It is shining into the darkness, but the darkness does not apprehend it. It is shining into the darkness, but the darkness is not overcoming it. It is shining in many a soul, and already the new order has begun within the kingdom of the heart. It is shining in many a small group and creating a heavenly-earthly fellowship of children of the light. It will always shine and lead many into the world of need, that they may bear it up into the heart of God.

Negative spaces can show us that the light for which we hunger in our darkest days is already shining. They show us that, if can we learn to look beyond and through the dark "positives" that seem to occupy all of our sight. Aldous Huxley wrote:

> We apprehend Him in the alternate voids and fullness of a cathedral; in the space that separates

the salient features of a picture; in the living geometry of a flower, a seashell, an animal; in the pauses and intervals between the notes of music, in their difference of tones and sonority; and finally, on the plane of conduct, in the love and gentleness, the confidence and humility, which give beauty to the relationships between human beings.

Voids and fullness surround us. Both are filled, strangely enough, with God's Light. Just as his ways are not our ways, neither is God's Light like our light. God's Light shines in emptiness *and* fullness.

ILLUMINATING MOMENT
Breathe deeply.
Relax your body and mind.
Think about the following slowly and gently.
Savor each thought.
What are the negative spaces in my life?
Do I see light in any of them?

It seemed obvious enough to me driving the MG that I'd want headlights to make a safe passage from Speedway to Plainfield. The problem on the country road that night, I found out as poked around under the bonnet the next day, was that the battery lead was corroded. It wasn't making a good connection. The power was there. The connection wasn't. The power couldn't get from the battery to the lights.

One way I try to stay connected to the Light is by having some time of personal worship every day. I've got books around me that remind me to do that. They vary from one day or month to the next—the *Book of Common Prayer*, *The Quiet Eye: A Way of Looking at Pictures*, John Baillie's *Diary of Private Prayer*, a New Testament, and so on.

Many of these aren't from my particular tradition. But each is rooted in deep Christian faith and imagination and so has something to teach me. For me, my best time is when I first get to the office. I pour some coffee and pick up one of the books and read a section. If I'm traveling, I do a variation on that theme. I get my coffee from the lobby, find a quiet spot, and read a piece for that day. That works for me now. It didn't five years ago.

There are other books, as well. Books, not surprisingly for a writer I guess, take up lots of space, physically, emotionally, and soulfully, in my life. One way I find new light through them is from the books of an obvious spiritual nature. The "Best of Spiritual Writing" series and pieces by Anne Lamott, Scott Russell Sanders, Kathleen Norris, and others nourish me. But so too does "nonspiritual" nonfiction and fiction—strong stories told by people who are wrestling with the great themes of life and faith. Reading helps me Mind the Light.

My friends often help me this way. One of the favorite games some friends of mine and I play when we're together (which is only a few times a year because we're all writers scattered around the country) is "what's the best book you've read recently?" or "what are the two books you'd take on a trip with you if you could only take two books?"

or variations of things like that. I always come home with ideas.

Another source of light for me is connection to a faith community. I do attend a local Friends meeting. I find a lot of help and support there. But my primary faith community is at work. I find my faith supported, challenged, and deepened by the people I work with. We do have a spiritual mission, that of helping connect congregations with resources so they can accomplish the tasks and mission they feel God has laid out for them. But what makes it a spiritual community for me is not the mission, it's the people. Each person there is a person of deep faith. It's not always a faith that's spoken aloud, but it is present in their lives. As we come to know each other—our beliefs, our cares, our joys, our sorrows—I find light for my journey. When Nancy's father died, these people of faith came to see us and care for us and uphold us. They lived out Edith Wharton's description of there being two ways of spreading light—"to be the candle or the mirror that reflects it." In this case, they both brought light and reflected God's Light.

Yet another source for me is spiritual music. For me it's not Christian radio with its pop sounds, it's more music like Robert Koopman's "Sacred Improvisations: Piano Improvisations on Hymns, Spirituals and Chants" or Iris DeMent's "Lifeline." I have a pretty big CD habit, something not in keeping with a Quaker testimony of simplicity, and it consists of a wide range of musical styles. The CDs I play at work, while writing, or traveling in airplanes tend to be the ones with the most obvious spiritual content. Sometimes it's overt like "Where The Sun Will Never Go

Down," Chanticleer's collection of spirituals, or John Rutter's "Requiem." At other times it's more subtle, such as Over the Rhine's "Changes Come": "There is all this untouched beauty / The light the dark both running through me / Is there still redemption for anyone / . . . Jesus come / Turn the world around."

Then there's poetry. My poet friend Mary Brown says that poetry is the only writing truly done to the glory of God. Partly, she says, that's true because writing poetry pays so poorly that you have to do it for God, because there's no reward coming from anywhere else. But even though there's a joke there, she's not entirely kidding. Poetry runs through the life of faith. Judaism gives us the Psalms. Christianity gave us the poetic expression of Mary, Elizabeth, Zacharias, John Donne, Hildegard of Bingen, John Bunyan, Gerald Manley Hopkins. Poetry has been written by all stripes of Christians. Even Quakers. We, who eschewed almost all other art forms in our early years, fearing they would distract us from learning of and from God, allowed poetry. One such early Quaker poet was Mary Mullineux. A Friend in a time of great persecution of our movement, Mullineux studied Latin, Greek, mathematics, and biology—at a time few folks, let alone women, did. And during her daily times of contemplation she wrote poetry, including these lines that must have come during times of trial, titled "Meditations in Trouble":

> How long, alas, my Love, my Life
> Wilt thou with-hold the influence
> Of thy enam'ring countenance,

The Light of Life! Bow down thine ear
To an afflicted heart, and hear
Its cries and groans, and grant relief.

Tis none but thee, thou Holy One!
Tis thy prevailing Light alone
Can rend the veil, and these clouds remove;
It's thou that grieves for me,
And makes my soul in sympathy,
Thus pant after thee, thou God of Love.

Today I glean light from the poems of Luci Shaw, Michael Dennis Browne, Sharron Singleton, David Craig, David Citino, Andrew Hudgins, and many more. I keep a file folder full of poems I've clipped out of various magazines and journals or read on the Internet. I pop these away and from time to time, especially on dark days (whether physically dark or spiritually dark), I take them out. I always find some that speak to my condition.

Poetry, music, literature, prayers, people. These are the things that bring light for my journey when I need light most. They keep me connected to the source of all art and light. Your Light List may be similar to mine—or completely different. You'll want to look at the things you've discovered that offer you light in dark times or speak to your Inner Light. Pay attention to them. They may be things that seem unconnected to the idea of light—yet, if they feed your soul, they are sources of luminosity for your life. And there is an old hymn that says:

We have but faith, we cannot know;
For knowledge is of things we see;
And yet we trust it comes from thee,
A beam in darkness; let it grow.

Pay attention to those things that nurture the beam in the darkness. Take light for your journey—a light that gives life to your soul.

ILLUMINATING MOMENT
Breathe deeply.
Relax your body and mind.
Think about the following slowly and gently.
Savor each thought.
What lights do I need for my journey?
Where will I find them?

"Oh, look at the sky," cried Nancy. It was a Sunday morning, and we stood in our bedroom, dressing for meeting for worship. For the better part of a week gray clouds had been so low that we felt encased in gloom. Three days earlier the sky had dumped eight inches of snow, and for the past two days winds of 30 to 45 mph had wiped our yard and fields clean of snow and left deep drifts in our driveway. Then came the break in the sky to which Nancy pointed. Clear blue all the way to the western horizon, which in our part of Indiana looks to be a long way away. The gloom lifted. Indirect light, since the opening hadn't reached the sun yet, flooded the fields. Then the sun broke through, flooding our world in dazzlement. Deer tracks stood out clearly against the snow along with the sight of birds fluttering up from the snow into the trees like leaves falling upward.

Nancy's face shown, too. Not just with light reflecting from the outside. But light deep inside. A beauty suffused her as she smiled and soaked in the light. Those too brief moments were a blessing.

Sometimes we Mind the Light by appreciating the natural light that surrounds, sustains, and reminds us of God. Sometimes it happens when we see others and behold God's Light within them shining out at us. Sometimes it comes from the companions we choose to light our way—music, poetry, art. Regardless, we will find our way home to and in God when we Mind the Light. As Andreas Feininger writes, "I am sure—as sure as anyone can be of anything—that in the end there will be light, an all-pervading insight illuminating the immense structure of the cosmos, revealing the rightful place and purpose of man."

Minding the Light is about blessing. Being blessed by God, "the father of all lights," and blessed by the creation lit by those lights. And in turn becoming a blessing to those around us as we pay witness to the light in them. Surely God has blessed us—every one.

ACKNOWLEDGMENTS

Oprah Winfrey once said, "Let your light shine—shine within you so that it can shine on someone else." People who let their lights shine within them so they could shine on me have been a blessing to me while I was writing this book. Tim Shapiro, a trustworthy friend and deep reader (and my boss), offered constant encouragement and advice. Likewise, Peggy Spohr, the Emma Peel of bookstores and libraries, read various drafts and offered detailed suggestions for improvements. Aaron Spiegel, my twin brother of a different mother, was my source for all things Jewish. Dr. Beth Groninger provided all sorts of insight—mostly during my eye exams—into how humans see. T. Canby Jones, my beloved college mentor, read through, and marked up, each page as carefully as he did my term papers thirty years ago.

I am especially grateful to some new friends—principally William Brosend, associate director of the Louisville Institute, and Don Ottenhoff, of the Ecumenical Institute at St. John's University and Seminary. Bill and Don hosted a group of writers at a "writer's asylum" in Collegeville, Minnesota. They, the other participating writers, and writing coach Cynthia Malone of the College of St. Benedict contributed greatly to this book. It was one of the great experiences of my writing life.

Lil Copan, my editor at Paraclete Press, is blessed with
wise eyes and a sensitive spirit. She uses both as she
encourages me to write clearly, creatively, and care-fully.
Thanks, Lil.

Of course, any mistakes in theology or clarity are mine—
not these lightbringers'.

Finally, there's Nancy. She's been my main teacher in
learning to appreciate the daily holiness of life. A woman of
deep faith and a centered heart, she encouraged my writing
and taking walks in the wood to take long looks. Her sharp
eyes also caught all the "a"s, "ands," and "the's" that I
thought I'd typed in, but had left out. For her love and keen
eyes, I'm grateful.

✳

Further Exercises in Seeing

The "Illuminating Moments" scattered throughout this book are based on the Friendly practice of asking "Queries." This custom began in the seventeenth century—hence the quaintness of the word Queries (though some Friends have taken to calling them "Questions for Spiritual Growth," which is clearer to most people, but just doesn't have the ring of "Queries"). Quakers don't have a formal creed or prayer book, so early Friends came up with the concept of asking individual and corporate questions as a way of gauging spiritual growth and health. The "Illuminating Moments" exercises are similar, except that instead of being rooted primarily in Quaker faith and life, they are drawn from wider Christian practice, history, and the Bible. They are a way to look, with attention and love, at how we can Mind the Light in our own lives.

The Illuminating Moments are a form of guided self-examination. They aren't meant to be a set of rules. There are no right answers. Use these further exercises in seeing in the same way as the Illuminating Moments sprinkled throughout the book—relax your body and mind, breathe deeply, put down the book, and use the opportunity to think slowly, gently, and soulfully.

Do I set aside times of deep looking for God?

Where do I see God at work (or play) today?

How is the Light of God at work in the ordinary activities and experience of my daily life?

Where I have seen creation imbued with God's spirit?

In what ways do I look for that of God within every person?

How have I gained a greater awareness of God's Light that is in us all?

Do I regularly read the Bible and other spiritual literature, looking for God's Light?

Do I see my time, talents, energy, money, material possessions, and other resources as gifts from God, to be held in trust and shared according to the Light I've been given?

Do I take time to talk with others about their experiences of the Light?

Do I heed the promptings of Light in my life?

Am I open to new light, from whatever source it may come?

Do I live adventurously, following the Light?

Some Resources for Minding the Light

Books

There are a number of books related to spirituality and deep seeing. Many of them are listed in the notes for each chapter. The list below is comprised of my favorites—each is a treasure.

God Is at Eye Level: Photography as a Healing Art by Jan Phillips (Wheaton, IL: Quest Books, 2000). My copy of Phillips's book is tattered—I enjoy it for both its photographs and its writing. The title is misleading, as the book is about "healing" only in its largest sense—recovering a healthy view of ourselves, others, the world, spirituality, and the abundance of daily life through looking at and taking photographs.

Our Hope for Years to Come: The Search for Spiritual Sanctuary by Martin Marty and Micah Marty (Minneapolis: Augsburg, 1995). This theologian father and his photographer son team up to provide meditations, photographs of American churches (from small prairie congregations to St. John the Divine in New York), and classic hymns that can be used as a guide for prayer and reflection. It's a wonderful blend of art and spiritual seeing.

A Private History of Awe by Scott Russell Sanders (New York: North Point Press, 2006). Sanders, the award-winning author of *Writing from the Center, The Force of Spirit, Hunting for Hope*, and many others, has written a moving book about recovering a sense of awe amidst the everyday experiences of life. It's truly a book about being spiritually sighted.

The Quiet Eye: A Way of Looking at Pictures by Sylvia Shaw Judson (Washington, D.C.: Regnery Publishing, 1982). Judson, a Quaker sculptor, combines art with text in a wonderful tiny book to help readers see the affirmation, wonder, and sacramental nature of daily life.

Workplace Spirituality

For information and practical helps about workplace spirituality, take a look at www.workplacespirituality.info. This website has articles and resources about the practice of spirituality in the workplace. It offers a wide range of topics from ethics to using spiritual values at work and offers an e-mail newsletter. Click on the topic of your interest.

Quakers and Quaker Spirituality

If you'd like to know more about Quakers and Quaker spirituality, visit Friends World Committee for Consultation—Section of the Americas (FWCC) at www.fwccamericas.org. Quakers are an incredibly diverse group of folks from all parts of the world. Friends are generally divided into two types—Programmed or

Unprogrammed. A programmed Friends meeting is one where worship has preplanned speaking and music. The majority of Friends congregations in the United States are either programmed or semi-programmed. Unprogrammed Friends meetings are the traditional "silent" meetings with no paid pastor or order of worship. This age-old Friends way of worship is still practiced in many meetings. FWCC has a Friends meeting or church locater (in case you'd like to visit one—guests are always welcome) and sponsors a group called The Wider Quaker Fellowship (WQF). The WQF is open to people of all faiths (or of no faith) who are interested in learning more about living Quakerism.

Notes

Introduction

p. 3 "My father loved first light." "Comeback" Tess Gallagher from *Dear Ghosts* (St. Paul, MN: Graywolf Press, 2006).

Chapter One

p. 8 "God is light; in him is no darkness at all." 1 John 1:5 (NIV).

p. 10 "Were the eye not of the sun. . . ." Johann Wolfgang von Goethe, quoted at wsrv.clas.virginia.edu/~rlk3p /desource/quotes.html.

p. 10 "who can say God has illumined me in both eyes. . . ." *Illuminations of Hildegard of Bingen*, 2nd ed. text by Hildegard of Bingen, commentary by Matthew Fox (Rochester, VT: Bear & Company; 2002).

p. 10 "When I judge art, I take my painting and put it next to a God-made object . . ." Paul Cézanne quoted at www.princetonol.com/groups/iad/lessons/middle/quotes.htm.

p. 13 "In the act of deeply seeing. . . ." Alex Grey, *The Mission of Art* (Boston: Shambhala, 1998), 72.

p. 14 "And God said, 'Let there be light,' and there was light. God saw that the light was good." Genesis 1:3-4 (NIV).

p. 14 "God made two great lights—the greater light to govern the day and the lesser light to govern the night." Genesis 1:16 (NIV).

p. 14 "God saw that [they were] good." Genesis 1:18 (NIV).

p. 15 "The true light, which enlightens everyone, was coming into the world." John 1:9 (NRSV).

p. 16 "While you have the light, believe in the light, so that you may become [children] of light." John 12:36 (RSV).

p. 16 "A people who walked in darkness has seen a great light." Isaiah 9:2 (RSV).

p. 16 "[W]alk as children of light (for the fruit of the light is found in all that is good and right and true)." Ephesians 5:8-9 (RSV).

p. 17 "It was a light that was so bright. . . ." Thomas Merton, *The Seven Storey Mountain* (New York: Harcourt Brace and Company, 1948, 1978), 311.

p. 18 "You never finish with it . . . ." Geraldine Brooks, "Unfinished Business: Jørn Utzon returns to the Sydney Opera House," *The New Yorker*, October 17, 2005, 98.

p. 19 "I guess I like the literal quality, or feeling, or sensation, in that I want to feel light physically." James Turrell, interview from the PBS series *Art:21*, www.pbs.org/art21 /artists/turrell/clip2.html.

p. 19 "We generally use [light] to illuminate other things" Robert Baldridge "Meeting the Light: An Interview with James Turrell," beliefnet.com/features/turrell.html.

p. 20 "Light I acknowledge as the energy upon which all life on this planet depends." Ruth Bernhard quoted at www.womeninphotography.org/ruthbernhardAA.html. Bernhard began work as a darkroom assistant but soon left New York (in 1935) to study under Edward Weston in California and later was a colleague of Ansel Adams, Imogen Cunningham, and Minor White.

p. 22 "I'd heard that Quakers have as many words for silence as Eskimos do for snow." Belden C. Lane, "Holy Silence: Invitation to Sabbath," *The Christian Century*, October 24, 2001.

p. 22 "One begins to suspect that the contemplation of any

ordinary thing, made extraordinary by attention and love. . . ." Belden C. Lane, "The Ordinary as Mask of the Holy," *The Christian Century*, October 3, 1984.

p. 23 "In silence which is active, the Inner Light begins to glow—a tiny spark. . . ." Pierre Lacout quoted in *Quaker Faith & Practice: The Book of Christian Discipline of the Yearly Meeting of the Religious Society of Friends (Quakers) in Britain*, 2nd ed., (London: Yearly Meeting of the Religious Society of Friends, 1995), 2:12.

CHAPTER TWO

p. 26 "Satan himself masquerades as an angel of light." 2 Corinthians 11:14 (NIV).

p. 29 "Every step in the process of taking pictures is a step toward the light, an experience of the holy, an encounter with the God who is at eye level, whose image I see wherever I look." Jan Phillips in *God Is at Eye Level: Photography as a Healing Art* (Wheaton, IL: Quest Books, 2000), 2.

p. 30 "The ultimate experience of anything is a realization of what's behind it." Minor White quoted by Jan Phillips in *God Is at Eye Level: Photography as a Healing Art* (Wheaton, IL: Quest Books, 2000), 21. Minor White was one of America's major post-World War II photographers. He worked as a photographer for the Works Progress Administration in Oregon while in his thirties and after the war studied with Edward Weston and Alfred Steiglitz. During this time, his photographs began to reflect his interest in spiritual concerns, primarily as found in Roman Catholicism, Zen Buddhism, and mysticism. White believed that taking and studying photographs were spiritual exercises. White was a deeply religious man whose whole life was a spiritual journey. For more on Minor White, see

www.profotos.com/education/referencedesk/masters/
masters/minorwhite/minorwhite.shtml.

p. 31 "the struggle through which a spark of true faith was lighted in my soul." Caroline Fox quoted in *Quaker Faith and Practice,* 2nd ed. (London: The Yearly Meeting of the Religious Society of Friends in Britain, 1995), 26.04.

p. 33 "If you do not see what is around you every day, what will you see when you go to Tangiers?" Freeman Patterson quoted by Jan Phillips in *God Is at Eye Level: Photography as a Healing Art* (Wheaton, IL: Quest Books, 2000), 59. Freeman Patterson, of New Brunswick, Canada, holds a Master of Divinity degree from Union Theological Seminary at Columbia University. This makes him one of the few theologically trained photographers in the world, if not the only one. His master's thesis was "Still Photography as a Medium of Religious Expression." Patterson says, "For me there is a close connection between art and religion in the sense that both are concerned about questions of meaning—if not about the meaning of existence generally, then certainly about the meaning of one's individual life and how a person relates to his or her total community/environment." His website is www.freemanpatterson.com.

p. 34 "My eyes find God everywhere, in every living thing, creature, person, in every act of kindness, act of nature, act of Grace." Jan Phillips, *God Is at Eye Level: Photography as a Healing Art* (Wheaton, IL: Quest Books, 2000), 80.

p. 34 "Whoever does not see God in every place does not see God in any place." Simcha Raz, ed. *Hasidic Wisdom: Sayings from the Jewish Sages* (Lanham, MD: Jason Aronson, 1998).

p. 42 "For the beauty of the earth. . . ." "For the Beauty of the Earth," words by Folliot Pierpoint, music by Conrad Kocher.

p. 42 "Nobody sees a flower really—it is so small it takes time—we haven't time—and to see takes time, like to have a friend takes time." Georgia O'Keeffe, quoted at www.artcyclopedia.com/artists/okeeffe_georgia.html.

p. 43 "God created light and he divided it into ten zones." Ansel Adams as quoted by Alain Briot, "How to Find the Best Light for a Specific Photograph," www.luminouslandscape.com /columns/composition-4.shtml.

p. 44 "Every generous act of giving, with every perfect gift, is from above, coming down from the Father of lights," James 1:17 (NRSV).

Chapter Three

p. 46 "Allah is the Light of the heavens and the earth . . . Light upon light, Allah guideth unto His light whom He will. . . . Allah is Knower of all things." The Qur'an as quoted in *Every Eye Beholds You*, Thomas J. Craughwell ed., (New York: Quality Paperback Book Club, 1998), 71.

p. 47 "Who is the Deity we shall worship with our offerings?" Hindu scripture as quoted in *Every Eye Beholds You*, Thomas J. Craughwell ed., (New York: Quality Paperback Book Club, 1998), 19.

p. 47 "I borrowed that word from the physical universe . . . If you shine a light on a translucent object, it appears to glow from within. . . ." Arjuna Ardagh as quoted in Deborah Caldwell, "The Translucent Revolution," www.beliefnet.com/story/175/story_17524_1.html.

p. 48 "Enlightenment is man's leaving his self-caused immaturity. . . ." Immanuel Kant, "What is Enlightenment?" essay written in 1784 and reprinted in *What is Enlightenment?: Eighteenth-Century Answers and Twentieth-Century Questions*, James Schmidt, ed., (Berkeley: University of California Press, 1996).

p. 45 "There is nothing new under the sun." Ecclesiastes 1:9 (NIV).

p. 46 "Test Your Enlightenment IQ," www.beliefnet.com /section/quiz/index.asp?sectionID=&surveyID=112.

p. 48 "Enlightenment, don't know what it is." "Enlightenment" from the album *Enlightenment* (words and music by Van Morrison) © 1990, Caledonia Publishing, Ltd.

p. 50 "Knowing only that God was present, he [Brother Lawrence] walked in the light of faith and was content just to lose himself in God's love no matter what happened." Brother Lawrence *The Practice Of the Presence Of God* (New Kensington, PA: Whitaker House, 1982), 17.

p. 50 "This incident turned on the light for me in the world that had grown very dark with futility. . . ." Agnes Sanford, *The Healing Light* (New York: Ballantine Books, 1972), 3-4.

p. 51 "The Way of Light is a spirituality of joy . . . [where] each exercise seeks to be exhilarating by reinforcing the clear New Testament teaching that spiritual life is an invitation to maximize joy despite deep pain. . . ." Mary Ford-Grabowsky, *Stations of the Light: Renewing the Ancient Christian Practice of the Via Lucis as a Spiritual Tool for Today* (New York: Image Books, 2005), 32.

p. 53 "There is one, even Christ Jesus, that can speak to thy condition." George Fox quoted in *Quaker Faith and Practice*, 2nd ed. (London: The Yearly Meeting of the Religious Society of Friends (Quakers) in Britain, 1995), 19:02.

p. 53 "There is a spirit which I feel that delights to do no evil, nor to revenge any wrong, but delights to endure all things, in hope to enjoy its own in the end." James Nayler quoted in *Quaker Faith and Practice*, 2nd ed. (London: The Yearly Meeting of the Religious Society of Friends (Quakers) in Britain, 1995), 19:12.

p. 55 "The true light which enlightens everyone. . . ." John 1:9 (NRSV).

p. 55 "O LORD, you have searched me and known me." Psalm 139:1-6 (NRSV).

p. 56 "the kind of mind that is willing to have its sense of mystery deepened by contact with reality. . . ." *Mystery and Manners: Occasional Prose by Flannery O'Connor* (New York: Farras, Straus and Geroux, 1969) 79.

p. 58 "Christ in you, the hope of glory." Colossians 1:27 (NRSV).

p. 59 "The eye with which I see God is the same as that with which God sees me. . . ." *Meister Eckhart* by Meister Eckhart (San Francisco: HarperSanFrancisco, 1957), 206.

p. 60 "When Aaron and all the Israelites saw Moses, the skin of his face was shining, and they were afraid to come near him" Exodus 34:30 (NRSV).

p. 60 "growing frame of wisdom, 'shining more and more unto the perfect day.'" from *Friends and God* by Mary K. Blackmar, cited at www.fgcquaker.org/library/welcome/fa-god.html.

p. 60 "You can light a virtual candle there and send a prayer request to the sisters." This website is at www.praythenews.com/LightA Candle.htm.

p. 62 "This is the message we have heard from him and proclaim to you, that God is light and in him is no darkness at all." 1 John 1:5 (NRSV).

p. 64 "The light that shows us our sins is the light that takes them away." George Fox as quoted in Roy Waddle, "Clutter Keeps Mounting," *The Tennessean*, November 5, 2005.

p. 64 "[that there was an ocean of darkness. . . . an infinite ocean of light. . . ." John N. Nickalls, ed. *Journal of George Fox* (London: Religious Society of Friends, 1975), 19.

p. 65 "All of us are like passengers strapped into the wildest ride at the amusement park. . . ." Garret Keizer, *A Dresser of Sycamore Trees* (Boston: Nonpareil Book, 2001), 67.

p. 68 "The branches outside this office window / too often block the light, but today the early/. . . ." Mary Brown, "Early Spring Aubade," © Mary Brown, 2005.

CHAPTER FOUR

p. 70 "[walk cheerfully over the world, answering that of God in everyone." George Fox as quoted in John N. Nickalls, ed., *Journal of George Fox* (London: Religious Society of Friends, 1975), 263.

p. 71 "Blessed art thou, Lord our God, King of the Universe, who dost vary the aspect of thy creatures." Quoted in Thomas J. Craughwell, ed, *Every Eye Beholds You*, (New York: Quality Paperback Book Club, 1998), 288.

p. 72 "Truly I tell you, just as you did it to one of the least of these who are members of my family, you did it to me." Matthew 25:40 (NRSV).

p. 74 "When the eyes see what they have never seen before, the heart feels what it has never felt." Baltasar Gracián quoted by Jan Phillips in *God Is at Eye Level: Photography as a Healing Art* (Wheaton, IL: Quest Books, 2000), 51. Gracián was a seventeenth-century Spanish Jesuit philosopher, scholar, satrist, philosopher, and writer who often found himself on the wrong side of Jesuit authority. He is best known today for his many sayings that have become epigrams.

p. 75 "I love mankind; it's people I can't stand." Robert L. Short, *The Gospel According to Peanuts* (New York: Bantam Books, 1968), 107.

p. 75 "As statements of core beliefs go, this is a good one: catchy, fairly simple, even biblically sound (see John 1:9)."

Thom Jeavons, "General Reflections: The Promise & the Challenge," *Philadelphia Yearly Meeting News*, September-October 2004 www.pym.org/pm/comments.php?id=1222_0_86_0_C.

p. 76 "Chariot from Hades, fire / glinting from its windshields. . . ." "Little Blessing Spoken in Road Rage," Jeanne Murray Walker, *The Christian Century*, January 25, 2005.

p. 77 "I hold up persons before God in intercession, loving and seeing them under God's eyes, longing for God's healing and redeeming power to course through their lives. . . ." Douglas Steere, "Quaker Meeting for Worship," www.pym.org/publish/pamphlets/qmw.htm.

p. 80 "Christ is always with us, always asking for room in our hearts. . . ." "Room for Christ" by Dorothy Day, *The Catholic Worker*, December 1945, p. 2.

p. 82 "And they tell her, one by one: A teacher helped me; there was a homeless person in the park; I saw a tree with lots of flowers." Dorothy C. Bass, *Receiving the Day: Christian Practices for Opening the Gift of Time* (San Francisco: Jossey-Bass, 2001), 15.

p. 82 ". . . makes no separation/just fiercely loves us all." "I Heard an Owl" Carrie Newcomer, BMI, copyright 2002, administered by Bug Music, from the album *The Gathering of Spirits* by Carrie Newcomer.

p. 83 "As kingfishers catch fire, dragonflies draw flame;" Gerald Manley Hopkins, "As Kingfishers Catch Fire, Dragonflies Draw Flame," www.bartleby.com/122/34.html. Hopkins was born in the mid-nineteenth century and won poetry prizes when he was in grammar school. At Oxford, he came under the influence of John Henry Newman (a former Anglican like himself) and converted to Catholicism. He soon joined the Society of Jesus and gave up poetry (even to the point of burning his early poems, feeling that poetry writing was too individualistic for a religious. After further study, he decided poetry was not incompatible with Jesuit principles.) He began writing poetry again, though most of it was not published until almost twenty years after his death.

p. 83 "This central affirmation, that the Light of the Christ-like God shines in every person, implies that our knowledge of God is both subjective and objective. . . ." L. Hugh Doncaster quoted in *Quaker Faith and Practice,* 2nd ed. (London: The Yearly Meeting of the Religious Society of Friends (Quakers) in Britain, 1995), 26.65.

CHAPTER FIVE

p. 86 "The impact of artificial light on nineteenth-century life was as profound as the impact of digital technology in the twentieth century." Ellen S. Wilson, "Light! The Industrial Age 1750–1900, Art & Science, Technology & Society," *Carnegie Magazine,* March–April 2001, www.carnegiemuseums.org/cmag/[bk_issue/2001/marapr/cma1.htm.

p. 87 [The easy availability of light ". . . got people thinking of light as a material, manipulatable thing, not a gift from God." Louise Lippincott as quoted in Ellen S. Wilson "Light! The Industrial Age" *Carnegie Magazine,* March–April2001,www.carnegiemuseums.org/cmag/bk_issue/2001/mrapr/cmal.htm.

p. 89 "We even fool the birds, which serenade false dawns caused by all sorts of bottled light." National Public Radio host Scott Simon referred to "the company that bottled light" in a story about General Electric. GE manufactures lightbulbs (and jet engines and home appliances and diesel locomotives and . . .). Scott Simon, "Jack Welch," *Weekend Edition,* December 2, 2000, www.npr.org/templates/story/story.php?storyId=1114826.

p. 90 "Study of a Winged Figure" by artist John Rush. This drypoint etching also appeared as the cover of my book *Imagination and Spirit: A Contemporary Quaker Reader* (Richmond, IN: Friends United Press, 2003). John's "Study of a Winged Figure" can be seen at www.johnrushillustration.com/h-pri/67-angel.html.

p. 98 "You just have to allow the light to reach your eyes." www.healthyplace.com/communities/bipolar/trillian/light_therapy.htm.

p. 99 "With further refinements, researchers think that light therapy can be used to destroy prostate cancer with few complications." ww.usaweekend.com/02_issues/021117/021117healthbriefs.html.

p. 99 "For this year, for the first time, it occurred to me that this annual explosion of light on people's front lawns and housetops is more than pretty or garish holiday decoration." Rev. C. Irving Cummings, "Reveling in the Dark," December 23, 2001, Old Cambridge Baptist Church, Cambridge, MA, www.oldcambridgebaptist.org/Sermons/revelingdark.html.

p. 101 "If you will try it out personally, observing the hours that govern the city clerk or laboring man, I believe that you will decide that God knows more about time than President Wilson does." C.W. Browne, *Scientific American,* October 18, 1919, 389.

CHAPTER SIX

p. 108 "When Jesus tells us about his Father, we distrust him." Emily Dickinson, quoted by Kathleen Norris in *The Cloister Walk* (New York: Riverhead Books, 1996), 27.

p. 109 "I came to realize that the best way to deepen my love of God was to use my experience of the love in my everyday life in all its variety, subtlety and uncertainty." John

Punshon, *Encounter with Silence: Reflections from the Quaker Tradition* (Richmond, IN: Friends United Press, 1987), 38.

p. 110 "On the morning of Frances' death, as I stood by her bedside, I made a secret resolve somewhere deep in my being which has only recently come to the surface." Zoe White quoted in *Quaker Faith & Practice,* 2nd ed. (London: The Yearly Meeting of the Religious Society of Friends (Quakers) in Britain, 1995), 22.87.

p. 111 "Where can I go from your Spirit?" Psalm 139:7, 11–12 (NIV).

p. 111 "A God we cannot be honest with is no God." Sheila Bovell quoted in *Quaker Faith & Practice,* 2nd ed. (London: The Yearly Meeting of the Religious Society of Friends (Quakers) in Britain, 1995), 22.83.

p. 112 "A neighbor gave me a battered old camera to take on my first trip abroad to Switzerland . . . ." Martin L. Smith, "Bearings: The Secret Darkroom of the Heart," *Washington Window*, vol. 73, no. 7, June 2005, http://www.edow.org /news/window/june2005/smith.html.

p. 115 "I am far from having arrived at the mount of vision where so many more faithful disciples have stood, above all mists of doubt." T. Edmund Harvey, quoted in *Quaker Faith & Practice,* 2nd ed.(London: The Yearly Meeting of the Religious Society of Friends (Quakers) in Britain, 1995), 26.48.

p. 116 "It is difficult for us to reconcile the two ideas of God as a loving Father and as the creator of all things, because of the existence of cruelty and undeserved suffering in Nature itself." Kathleen Lonsdale quoted by Anne Thomas, "This I Know Experimentally," Pendle Hill Quaker Study Center, Wallingford, PA Spring 2000, Monday Night Lecture Series, www.pendlehill.org/resources/files/lectures/04-27-200: pdf.

p. 118 "There's an ambiguity in the terms positive and negative space, since the two go together. . . ." Lucia A. Salemme, *Color Exercises for the Painter* (New York: Watson-Guptill Publications, 1970), 80.

p. 118 "Pushing for Life" is a mostly solid smooth limestone sculpture about five-feet high by two-feet wide and four to five inches deep. . . ." "Pushing for Life" and other Schiefer pieces can be viewed www.scican.net/~schiefer/family.html.

p. 122 "The light for which the world longs is already shining." Thomas R. Kelly, quoted in *Quaker Faith & Practice,* 2nd ed. (London: The Yearly Meeting of the Religious Society of Friends (Quakers) in Britain, 1995), 26: 62.

p. 122 "We apprehend Him in the alternate voids and fullness of a cathedral. . . ." Aldous Huxley, quoted by Jan Phillips in *God Is at Eye Level: Photography as a Healing Art* (Wheaton, IL: Quest Books, 2000), 5.

p. 125 "to be the candle or the mirror that reflects it." Edith Wharton, cited at http://www.edithwharton.org/events/6.php.

p. 126 "There is all this untouched beauty / The light the dark both running through me. . . ." "Changes Come," words by Karin Bergquist and Linford Detweiler, music by Karin Bergqist, Scampering Songs Publishing (ASCAP)/Nett Music (ASCAP) c/o Nettwerk Songs Publishing, Ltd., from the album *Ohio* by Over the Rhine.

p. 126 "How long, alas, my Love, my Life. . . . " W. Arthur Turner, ed., *Pathways to the Light Within: A Gathering of Early Quaker Poets* (Richmond, IN: Friends United Press, n.d.), 56.

p. 128 "We have but faith, we cannot know." "Strong Son of God, Immortal Love," words by Alfred Lord Tennyson, music by George Elvey, words from the poem "In

Memoriam A.H.H.," written in memory of his close friend Arthur Henry Hallam, who died when Tennyson was twenty-four years old.

p. 129 "I am sure—as sure as anyone can be of anything—that in the end there will be light, an all-pervading insight illuminating the immense structure of the cosmos, revealing the rightful place and purpose of man." Photographer Andreas Feininger, quoted by Jan Phillips in *God Is at Eye Level: Photography as a Healing Art* (Wheaton, IL: Quest Books, 2000), 137.

About Paraclete Press

Who We Are

Paraclete Press is an ecumenical publisher of books and recordings on Christian spirituality. Our publishing represents a full expression of Christian belief and practice—from Catholic to Evangelical, from Protestant to Orthodox.

Paraclete Press is the publishing arm of the Community of Jesus, an ecumenical monastic community in the Benedictine tradition. As such, we are uniquely positioned in the marketplace without connection to a large corporation and with informal relationships to many branches and denominations of faith.

We like it best when people buy our books from booksellers, our partners in successfully reaching as wide an audience as possible.

What We Are Doing

Books

Paraclete Press publishes books that show the richness and depth of what it means to be Christian. Although Benedictine spirituality is at the heart of all that we do, we publish books that reflect the Christian experience across many cultures, time periods, and houses of worship.

We publish books that nourish the vibrant life of the church and its people—books about spiritual practice, formation, history, ideas, and customs.

We have several different series of books within Paraclete Press, including the bestselling *Living Library* series of modernized classic texts; *A Voice from the Monastery*—giving voice to men and women monastics about what it means to live a spiritual life today; award-winning literary faith fiction; and books that explore Judaism and Islam and discover how these faiths inform Christian thought and practice.

Recordings

From Gregorian chant to contemporary American choral works, our music recordings celebrate the richness of sacred choral music through the centuries. Paraclete is proud to distribute the recordings of the internationally acclaimed choir Gloriæ Dei Cantores, who have been praised for their "rapt and fathomless spiritual intensity" by *American Record Guide*, and the Gloriæ Dei Cantores Schola, which specializes in the study and performance of Gregorian chant. Paraclete is also the exclusive North American distributor of the Monastic Choir of St. Peter's Abbey in Solesmes, France, long considered to be a leading authority on Gregorian chant performance.

Learn more about us at our Web site:
www.paracletepress.com, or call us toll-free at
1-800-451-5006.

ALSO BY J. BRENT BILL

Holy Silence
The Gift of Quaker Spirituality

Trade Paper
ISBN: 1-55725-420-6, $14.95

People of all faiths and back-
grounds are drawn to silence. We
yearn for it in these busy and difficult
times, but often, when silence
becomes available, we don't know
what to do with it.
For centuries, Quakers have taught that when we are silent,
God grants us insights, guidance, and spiritual understanding
that is different from what we might realize in our noisy, everyday lives. This wise book invites us to discover this and other
unique gifts of the Quaker way. It is a satisfying experience and
taste of a spiritual tradition unflinching in its dedication to
listening for the sounds and voice of God.

"Brent Bill reminds us that silence is a dwindling resource that
needs to be preserved for the sake of our souls. If you are seeking
to hear God's spirit beyond the din, follow the instructions it
offers. Relax your body and mind.
Breathe deeply. Pick up this book. And read.
Can you imagine how silence might change your life?"
—Diana Butler Bass, author of *Strength for the Journey:
A Pilgrimage of Faith in Community*

"A quietly lovely book in a hasty, clanging world.
Holy Silence is a cooling balm."
—Philip Gulley, author of the *Harmony* series

Available from most booksellers or through Paraclete Press:
www.paracletepress.com 1-800-451-5006.
Try your local bookstore first.